BOOK G
BASIC READING

GLENN McCRACKEN
New Castle, Pennsylvania

CHARLES C. WALCUTT
Queens College, Flushing, New York

J. B. LIPPINCOTT COMPANY
PHILADELPHIA, NEW YORK

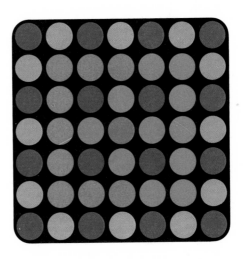

CONTENTS

Part 1—Famous Women

Part 2—Fun and Fantasy

Copyright ©, 1975, 1970, 1964 by J. B. Lippincott Company
Printed in the United States of America
International Rights Reserved
ISBN–0–397–43565–7

25.799.7

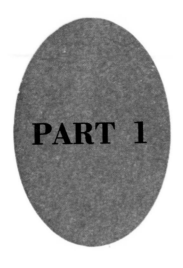

PART 1

Famous Women

Mercy Otis Warren

"Hannah, Hannah!" called Mercy. She raced up the stairs and into the bedroom that the two girls shared. Her long skirt was gathered up in her hands. The lace cap had fallen from her head, and her brown curls bounced about freely. "I'm going, Hannah!"

"Where, Mercy?" Hannah asked. She dropped the napkin she'd been sewing. "Are you going to town? To Plymouth? Surely not to Boston!" Any trip away from the Otis farm in Barnstable, Massachusetts, was a special event, but to go to the big city of Boston!

"Wait!" Mercy said, taking a deep breath. She was so excited she couldn't speak.

2

"What is it? Where are you going, Mercy?" Hannah asked. She was getting impatient. Hannah picked up the napkin and studied the tiny stitches she'd been practicing. In 1744, it was important for a young girl to learn to sew neatly. "Too bad Mercy doesn't like to sew," Hannah thought. "Mercy likes to spend all her time reading books or scribbling on pieces of paper."

Finally Mercy cried out, "I'm going to Harvard! Mother and Father said I may go with them to see James graduate from Harvard College! Hannah, isn't it wonderful?"

Hannah smiled at Mercy. "Yes, it is, but I wonder why I can't go."

"Don't forget, Hannah, you are only fourteen years old," Mercy said. "I am almost sixteen. That is old enough to get married, if I want to. Which I do not." Mercy looked for another lace cap and placed it over her curls. She smoothed her dress and put a fresh shawl around her shoulders. She looked tidy again, although the bright spots of red on her cheeks and her shining dark eyes gave away her excitement.

"I suppose you are right," said Hannah. "After all, you are James's best friend in the whole world. He has written more letters to you than to all the rest of us." Then she added softly, "And I know how much you've missed him these four years while he's been away at college. Anyway, I prefer to stay home. I do not like long trips. James will soon be home, and I want to prepare a special welcome for him. I will decorate the house and sew a surprise for him while you are gone. He knows me, and I am sure he will appreciate my own way of showing how proud I am of him."

The Otis Family

People often had very large families in Colonial times. With a large farm and a big house—and no machines run by gasoline or electricity—the thirteen children of the Otis family always had plenty of work to do. There were many servants, too, so that the farm was a little community. The Otis children played with the servants' children. Of all the sisters and brothers, Mercy and James were the closest friends.

Many visitors came to the big farm in Barnstable. Mr. Otis encouraged the three oldest children, James, Joseph, and Mercy, to gather round the great fire in the evenings and take part in the long conversations with their guests. Thus they learned about people and about the world. The children all learned to read at home, and their father kept the house well provided with books, newspapers, almanacs, and magazines. In those times there was more work than today, and there was also much more time for reading and talking, since these were people's main pleasures.

Mr. Otis sent his children every morning to the nearby home of the Reverend Jonathan Russell, for special lessons in language,

arithmetic, and history. James and Mercy, who always worked together, were his best students. History was Mercy's favorite subject. She read constantly in the history books that she borrowed from Mr. Russell's library.

Mercy learned that America was not a united country then, but thirteen separate colonies that were "owned" and ruled by Britain. From far across the ocean the British government sent a governor who had complete power over the people. But already some of the colonies were unhappy about being ruled from Britain, and some of them, like Massachusetts, were becoming very independent in their thinking. Later, when the colonies were fighting together for their independence from Britain, Mercy remembered what she had read as a young girl.

James went to Harvard College when he was fourteen. Mercy missed studying history with him almost as much as she missed his company. Indeed, history and James were hard to separate in her thoughts. James sent her books so that she could keep on

7

studying. Mr. Otis encouraged his girls to study, although in those times most people thought that girls should learn only how to sew and perform domestic chores.

Graduation Day

When it was time for James's graduation, Mercy could not contain her excitement. She didn't care about the boat trip to Boston and then the carriage ride to Harvard. She was only excited about seeing her brother James and the famous college he had told her so much about.

When Mercy and her parents finally got to Harvard, Mercy hugged James tightly. She was so glad to see him! Then Mercy tried to see everything that was going on. It was like a grand picnic. She met many of the proud students and saw the important visitors. She saw the governor and the judges. They were dressed in long dark gowns and wore puffy white wigs.

The day was long and full. Mercy listened to speeches by the visitors. She saw the

college diplomas presented to each young man who was graduating. With a great thrill she watched James step up to the stage, bow, and accept his diploma.

"Some day James will be as important as any visitor here," Mercy whispered to her mother beside her. "I just know it."

Mrs. Otis smiled at her daughter. For a minute she wished Mercy could earn a college diploma, too, but that was silly. No girls went to college in those days. It was thought that girls' brains were too weak for learning!

As the wonderful day came to an end, James Otis called his sister aside. "Mercy, there is someone I want you to meet. He is a friend of mine who is going to graduate next year."

Beside James stood a tall, handsome young man. His name was James Warren, and ten years from that time, he and Mercy Otis would be married.

Mercy Otis Becomes Mercy Otis Warren

Mercy's life didn't change much when she married James Warren. They lived in a fine, tall house in Plymouth, Massachusetts. Like those of her childhood home, the doors of

the Warren house were always open to visitors.

Mercy still loved history, but now she was helping to make history. The visitors to the Warren home were Americans who wanted their country to be free from Britain. As they gathered before Mercy's fireplace, the icy New England wind whistled outside. Inside, the house burned hot with excitement as Mercy and her friends made plans for American freedom.

"What makes me so angry," said Mercy's brother, James, at one meeting, "is the way British officers can just walk into anyone's home or shop, whenever they want."

"To me," Mercy said, "the most unfair law of all is that we Americans must buy everything we need from Britain. I am going to have all the women band together and stop buying anything made in Britain. We will make our own clothes. We will grow our own food. We will even stop drinking tea!"

"Maybe that's going too far," her husband laughed. "I don't know whether I can give up my morning tea. Even if it *is* British!"

11

Mercy did not laugh. "You must learn to do without it, James," she said. But she knew she would miss her tea, too, and the beautiful clothes and furniture that rich Americans bought from Britain. But she wanted to fight this law. "If something cannot be made or grown in America," said Mercy, "we must learn to do without it."

Mercy and her friends wanted America to rule itself. They were called patriots, and James Otis was one of their leaders. Other Americans wanted to stay under British rule. Because they were loyal to Britain, they were called Loyalists or Tories. One night in 1769, James Otis was attacked by his Tory enemies. He was badly beaten, and he never got well.

Mercy was upset and very angry. She felt that now it was her duty to take her brother's place. She too could fight for freedom. She could fight by writing. She wrote poetry and plays that poked fun at the British. But she did not sign her name. Women in those days certainly did not sign their names to this kind of writing. It was, in fact, almost un-heard-of for them to do any public writing at all. Most women wrote pretty letters or poems about flowers and trees; but Mercy wrote about history and the government, and this made her a real pioneer in her time.

Many people read what Mercy wrote. Some liked her writings; others did not.

Her most famous play was called *The Group*. In it she said that the British were going to march out of Boston and head for the town of Concord. This is where the patriots hid their supplies. In fact, this is what happened! When the British marched out of Boston to take the supplies, the patriots tried to stop them. A small battle followed. This was called the Battle of Lexington and Concord, and it was the first battle for American freedom. It happened on April 19, 1775.

Mercy wrote other plays. But she never saw any of them acted on the stage. She wrote them only to be read and enjoyed by her friends.

Two of Mercy's closest friends were John and Abigail Adams. Mercy and Abigail would meet as often as they could. They both loved to read, and they would discuss books that had interested them. They also talked about their children and education. Mercy had five children, all boys.

"I wish I could teach my children more," Mercy once told Abigail. "So many of their lessons are left to me, and I know so little."

"It's the same with all women," said Abigail. "Mothers are supposed to teach their children, yet we do not get to go to school ourselves."

"There are so many things women are not allowed to do," said Mercy. "According to the law, my husband owns my plays and poems and he would be entitled to any money they earned."

"Women cannot legally own anything," Abigail told her. "When we are free from Britain, we women must try to win the rights that only men have now."

15

Although Mercy's plays and poems were famous, she is best known for the history book she wrote. In it she told about the war for American freedom. She wrote about the people who took part in the war. She told what happened when the war was over. It was a long, hard history to write, and it took Mercy twenty-five years to complete. When it was done, Mercy Otis Warren was proud. She had played an important part in the fight her brother James had begun so many years before. This was the fight for American freedom.

Maria Mitchell

It was February, 1831. The day was cold and clear. But on Nantucket Island, Massachusetts, not one person was seen in the streets. They were at home, watching the sky.

The Nantucket people depended on the sea. They were mostly fishermen, whalers, and traders. Watching the sky was important to them. The stars, sun, clouds, and moon told them about the weather and directions.

Today everyone was waiting for a rare event. An eclipse was coming. During a solar eclipse the moon moves between the earth and the sun. At one point the moon almost completely blocks out the sun.

In one of the houses, 12-year-old Maria Mitchell stood quietly beside her father. She was excited, but she was still. This was a very special day for Maria. Her father had chosen her to time the eclipse.

It was important for Maria to be quiet. Her father was setting up the telescope. He lifted out a windowpane. Through the space he carefully aimed the family telescope.

"Get ready to count now, Maria," said her father, peering through the telescope.

Maria's eyes were fixed on the clock. When her father gave the signal, Maria began to count. The eclipse lasted just over two minutes. Afterward Maria felt strange.

"Now I really feel like part of the sky and earth," Maria said to her father. "I can't explain it. I only know that I want to learn all about the sky."

That was the day Maria Mitchell decided to become an astronomer.

The Mitchell Family

Maria was born at a time when most girls learned only about housework. Maria was very good at housework. She liked to put everything exactly in its own place. Sometimes her four brothers and sisters joked about that.

"Maria is so fussy. Everything has to be in order," her oldest brother, Andrew, teased.

"There's nothing wrong with order," said Maria. "Look how orderly the sky is. Every star is in its special place."

Maria's family liked to read, talk, and learn. Her father was a teacher who loved astronomy. He was interested in what was happening in the sky. Her mother, Lydia, was interested in what was happening on earth. Maria was a little bit like each of them. She loved mathematics. That was important in studying the sky. And like her mother, she wanted to know what was happening around her.

When Maria was 16 years old, she became a teacher. She even ran her own school for a few months. Then she found a new job in a library. This was just perfect for Maria.

The library was open only on afternoons and Saturday nights. This left the mornings for Maria's housework. Her nights were for watching the sky.

They were long, hard days. Luckily Maria was always strong and healthy. She took long walks every day, even when the summers were hot and the winters were snowy.

Then on the night of October 1, 1847, her life changed. Maria Mitchell found something new in the sky. She found something that had not been there before.

Maria's Comet

It was already cold in October. But it was a perfect night for "sweeping the sky" with her telescope. There were no clouds and no wind.

Maria climbed up on the rooftop. She was wrapped up in a large, heavy coat. In one hand, she held her whale-oil lantern. She was all alone. Her father was downstairs with a visitor. Everything was very still. The calm night covered Maria like a blanket. Soon she did not even feel the cold.

Then, suddenly she cried, "What's this?"

She saw a strange, pale light. Maria knew the sky well. A new light was there that had not been there before.

Softly, Maria crept downstairs. She had to get her father. She did not dare let her excitement show. She might explode!

Maria's father looked through the telescope.

"Could it . . . could it be a comet?" Maria asked softly.

When her father looked up, he was smiling. "Yes, I'm sure it's a comet. This is wonderful, Maria. Do you know that the King of Denmark has promised a gold medal to anyone who discovers a new comet? I must write to him at once."

In the next few days, the new comet was seen by other astronomers all around the world. But Maria had been the first to spot it. She got the gold medal. She also became famous. Everyone knew her name. She was asked to join science clubs. She received prizes. Not only was she a "lady astronomer," but she was one of the few people to discover a comet.

Maria took a trip to Europe. When she came home, she had two surprises. One was a new telescope. It was given to her by a women's club. The other surprise was a job.

Maria, the Teacher

A new school was opening for women. It was named Vassar Female College. Maria was asked to be the astronomy teacher. There she worked for the rest of her life.

Maria was a good teacher. She wanted her students to understand the sky. When an exciting event was to take place, Maria made sure her students saw it. Even if it was in the middle of the night.

"Get up, get up!" Maria said one night, knocking on each girl's door.

One by one, the sleepy girls put on their coats. Slowly they met in the hall.

"It's freezing," one student said to her friend. "I wish Miss Mitchell would let us miss some of these events. It's so cold and so late."

"It's two o'clock in the morning!" another student said, as they climbed up on the roof.

But when they looked through the telescope, the students became as excited as their teacher. They saw hundreds of meteors racing across the sky. It looked like a silver rainfall.

"I never saw anything like this," said one student.

"It's beautiful," said another.

When the sight was over, Maria led the shivering girls downstairs.

"Sit here near the fire," she said. "I will bring some hot cocoa to warm us."

Sometimes, early in the morning, Maria called the girls to the roof. There they found little tables set for breakfast. The students liked to take turns eating hot toast and coffee and peering through the telescope.

Maria liked teaching the girls. She wanted women to enjoy school and work.

"I believe in women even more than I do in astronomy," she once said.

Maria received many honors. Her comet was called, "Miss Mitchell's Comet." A moon crater was named for her. Her name is carved with the names of other great Americans on the front of the Boston Library. Maria Mitchell proved how much women can do.

Sojourner Truth

It was raining hard that night over a hundred years ago. The rain dashed against the high windows of a church that was filled with people. On the platform behind the pulpit sat a group of women. The people in the church had come from miles around to hear the women speak for equal rights.

The crowd was noisy. Some men were stamping their feet and yelling at the stage, "Women have enough rights!"

One man yelled, "If you have equal rights, who will open doors for you? Who will give you his chair? Who will help you over a mud puddle?" Children in the crowd giggled. Men laughed and stamped their feet. None of the women on the platform stood up. No one wanted to be first to face the unfriendly men.

At one corner of the stage sat a black woman. She was staring at the floor. Through all the yelling, she had not moved once. She had never even lifted her head. But now she stood up.

"Don't let her speak," someone whispered, but she walked slowly across the stage, close to the men. She was almost six feet tall. She wore a long, plain dress that came down to her feet. It was gray and still damp with rain. She untied the strings of her bonnet, removed it from her head, and carefully placed it on a chair. Then she turned back to the audience.

The crowd suddenly became very quiet. When all eyes were upon her, the tall black woman began to speak. Her voice was rich

and deep. She did not speak perfectly, but everyone understood her.

"That man says that women needs to be helped into carriages and over ditches and have the best place everywhere. Nobody ever helps me into carriages or over mud puddles or gives me any best place—and ain't I a woman?"

Her voice rose till it filled the whole church. "Look at me! Look at my arm!" She raised an arm larger and stronger than most of the men there had. "I could work as hard as any man and eat as much, when I could get it . . ."

When she finished, the audience stood up and clapped. Someone called, "What is your name?"

"It's Sojourner Truth," she said. "Sojourner, because I roam all over the country; Truth, because that is my message."

Sojourner Truth had many messages of truth. That night she had talked about the way women were treated at the time. Women could not vote. Most colleges would not accept women. If they got married, they could not even own the clothes they wore. They could not keep the money they made working.

Sojourner Fights for Women's Rights

Sojourner believed that all people should be free. Women were not free. She felt they should demand the same rights that men had. Sojourner was a simple woman. She never went to school. She couldn't read or write. But she knew that women, like men, should try to get as much as they could out of life. When Sojourner finished speaking that night, the people in the audience admired her.

As the years passed, there were more meetings for the rights of women. At one meeting, even more men in the audience were rude. They cackled and hissed at the women who spoke. It sounded like a barnyard full of chickens and geese. Sojourner rose and came forward. Her courage was stronger than her fear of the crowd. Her voice was louder than the cackling and hissing before her. As she spoke, her eyes blazed with anger, and the noisy people suddenly became silent. Then someone at the back began stamping his feet and shouting, but Sojourner kept on speaking. Her voice was deep and powerful.

"I see that some of you have got the spirit of a goose, and some have got the spirit of a snake."

The men were startled. They did not know whether to make louder noises, or to let this brave woman be heard. Sojourner smiled, and the men smiled back at her. As angry as they were, everyone had to laugh. They **did** sound like geese and snakes.

But Sojourner didn't want to be friendly. She turned fierce and boomed out, "Don't you hear how some hiss their mothers like snakes? . . . Sons ought to behave themselves before their mothers, but I can see them a-laughing and pointing at their mothers up here on the stage. They hiss when an aged woman comes forth."

Sojourner told the men that being rude to her was the same as being rude to their own mothers. She made them feel ashamed. They listened to Sojourner as she told them about her life. Olive Gilbert, a woman working to stop slavery, had helped Sojourner write the story of her life—how she had been a slave in New York State; how she had run away when she was grown; how she journeyed hundreds of miles to tell her story. She had a magic quality that made people listen when she spoke. She proved that a slave could become an important person. In time, a great many people had heard of Sojourner, even Abraham Lincoln, the President of the United States.

Sojourner Meets the President

Once Sojourner visited the White House. She told Mr. Lincoln that she had never heard his name until he became President.

"But I had heard of you before I was President," said Mr. Lincoln.

Sojourner wanted to meet another famous person, Harriet Beecher Stowe, who had written a book that was being talked about all over the country. The book, *Uncle Tom's Cabin,* was about slavery, and it made many people see that slavery was wrong. Sojourner said, "I have to meet the woman who wrote that book."

Sojourner went to the Stowe home in Maine. The house was filled with visitors when she knocked at the door. Mrs. Stowe was polite to Sojourner. However, she didn't want to spend too much time with her because there were other, more famous guests waiting inside for her.

But Mrs. Stowe listened in the doorway to Sojourner—and she couldn't stop listening.

She fell under the magic of the woman's voice and eyes. Then she brought Sojourner into the living room, so all the people could hear her. Like children, they gathered around her, and listened as she spoke about slavery, freedom, honesty, truth, and equal rights for all people.

Sojourner stayed at the Stowe home for several days, and then she set forth again on her endless journey. She had so many people to talk to that she couldn't stop anywhere for long.

It was said that Sojourner was 105 years old when she died. Although she did not live to see women vote, Sojourner did see women win many rights. She saw them able to go to schools and colleges. She saw them get better jobs and keep the money they earned.

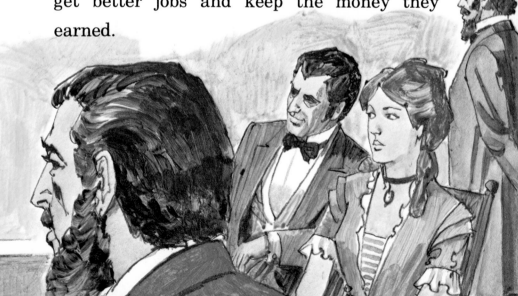

Roads Go Ever On and On

Roads go ever on and on,
  Over rock and under tree,
By caves where sun has never shone,
  By streams that never find the sea;
Over snow by winter sown,
  And through the merry flowers of June,
Over grass and over stone,
  And under mountains in the moon.

—*J. R. R. Tolkien*

38

Ask a Daffodil

Ask a daffodil
To trumpet
To the sun
That the time
For buds
To open
Has begun!

Ask a robin come
From lands
Beyond
The sun
To tell us all
That April
Has begun!
—*Adele H. Seronde*

39

The Aristocratic Snail

Underneath a cattail,
By the garden wall,
Lives a very rich old snail
Who never works at all.
His soap smells sweet like mother's
(Which I would love to use);
He never even bothers
To read the daily news.
He smokes a big long meerschaum pipe;
He eats the tenderest greens,
And never has to sweep, or wipe
The dishes, or pick the beans.
He just gets fatter every day
Because he has no rent to pay.

—*Monroe Stearns*

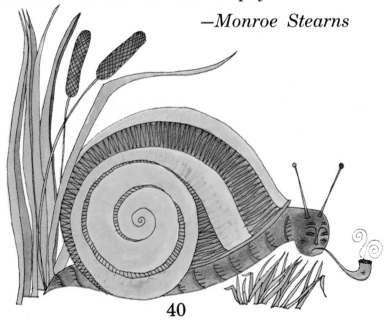

PART 2

Fun and Fantasy

Hansel and Gretel

Long ago a woodcutter lived with his wife and two children near the edge of a forest. The children were a boy named Hansel and his sister, Gretel. They were so poor that sometimes they did not have enough to eat.

One evening, after the children had gone to bed, the parents sat talking about their trouble. The husband said to his wife, who was not the mother of his children, but their stepmother, "What can we do? I cannot earn enough to buy food for you and me and the two children. What will we do with Hansel and Gretel? They must not starve."

"I know what to do, husband," said the wife. "Early tomorrow morning we will take the children for a walk into the forest, and we will leave them in the thickest part. They will never find their way home again. Then we will have to feed only ourselves."

"No, wife," said the man. "I will never do that. How could I leave my children in the woods where wild animals would get them?"

The wife kept trying to get her husband to agree to her plan. She let him have no rest until he became quite worn out. But he could not sleep for hours. He just lay thinking in sorrow about his children.

The two children, who were too hungry to sleep, heard all that their stepmother had said to their father. Poor little Gretel cried bitter tears as she listened. Then she said to her brother, "What is going to happen to us, Hansel?"

"Hush, Gretel," he whispered, "don't be so unhappy. I know what to do."

Then the children lay quite still until their parents were asleep. As soon as both parents were asleep, Hansel got up. He put on his little coat and slipped out of the door into the front yard. The moon shone brightly and the white pebble stones which lay in front of the cottage door glistened like new silver money. Hansel stooped and picked up as many of the pebbles as he could stuff in his little coat pockets. Then he went back to Gretel and said, "Don't worry, sister, I will take care of you." Then the children slept until morning.

A Trip into the Forest

As soon as the sun came up in the morning, the stepmother came and woke the children. She said, "Get up, you lazy bones, and come into the forest with me to gather wood for the fire." Then she gave each of them a piece of bread. She said, "You must keep that to eat for dinner, for you will get nothing more."

The stepmother started to lead the children deep into the forest. They had gone only a short distance when Hansel looked back at the house. He stopped and looked back again and again.

At last his stepmother said, "Why do you stay behind?"

"Oh, Mother," said the boy, "I can see my little white cat sitting on the roof of the house, and I am sure she is crying for me."

"Nonsense," replied the stepmother. "That is not your cat. It is the morning sun shining on the chimney."

Hansel had not seen a cat at all. He had wanted to stay behind as they walked so that he could drop the white pebbles from his pocket on the ground.

As soon as they reached a thick part of the forest, the stepmother said, "Come, children, gather some wood. I will make a fire, for it is very cold here."

Hansel and Gretel gathered quite a high pile of wood, which soon blazed into a bright fire.

Then the woman said to them, "Sit down here, children, and rest while I go to find your father. He is cutting wood in another part of the forest. When we have finished our work, we will come to take you home."

Hansel and Gretel rested themselves near the fire. When noon arrived, they each ate the pieces of bread that their stepmother had given them for their dinner.

As long as they heard the strokes of the ax they felt safe, for they thought their father was working near them. But it was not the ax they heard. It was only a branch which hung on a dead tree and was moved up and down against the tree trunk by the wind.

At last, when they had been sitting there a long time, the children became tired and they fell fast asleep. When they awoke, it was night, and poor Gretel began to cry. She said, "Oh, how shall we ever get out of the forest?"

"Don't be afraid," said Hansel. "We will wait a little while until the moon rises. Then we shall easily find our way home."

Very soon a full moon rose in the sky. Hansel took his little sister by the hand and started home. The white pebble stones he had dropped along the way glittered in the moonlight. That is how he knew which way to go. They walked all night and reached home just at the break of day.

They knocked at the door and when the stepmother opened it, she exclaimed, "'You naughty children, why did you stay so long in the forest? We thought you were never coming back." But their father was very sad to think that they had been left alone in the forest.

Not long after this, the children were in bed one night and they heard their stepmother talking again. She said to their father, "We are poorer than ever now. We have just half a loaf of bread left. The children must go away, for we cannot feed them any longer. This time we will take them deep into the forest, and they will not be able to find their way home as they did before." But the husband felt very sad again. He thought it was better to share the last bit of bread with his children.

His wife would not listen to him. She made plans to take the children deep into the forest the next morning.

Hansel and Gretel were awake and heard what their stepmother said. As soon as the parents were asleep, Hansel got up to go gather more white pebbles to drop as he walked so that he and his sister could follow them back home again. But his stepmother had locked the door, and he could not open it.

Lost in the Woods

Early the next morning the stepmother came and pulled the children out of bed. When they were dressed, she gave each of them a piece of bread for his dinner, smaller than they had had before. Then they started on their way to the forest.

Hansel did not have any white pebbles to drop along the way this time, so he broke off little crumbs from his piece of bread and dropped them. He thought he and Gretel could follow the crumbs and find their way back home.

They walked until they reached the thickest and deepest part of the forest, where they had never been before in all their lives. Again they made a big fire. Then their stepmother said, "Stay here, children, and rest while I go help your father cut wood. When we finish in the evening we will come and take you home."

The children sat around the warm fire until noon. Then Gretel shared her piece of bread with Hansel, for he had scattered his along the road as they walked. After this they slept for a while; evening came, but no

one had come to take them home. When
they awoke it was quite dark, and poor little
Gretel was afraid.

Hansel told her not to worry. "You know,
little sister," he said, "that I have thrown
bread crumbs all along the road as we traveled to get here. We can follow them back
home."

But when they went out of the bushes
into the moonlight, they found no bread
crumbs. The birds had picked them up.

Hansel tried to hide his fears when he
made this sad discovery. He said to his sister, "Cheer up, Gretel. We will find our
way home without the crumbs. Let's try."

They walked the whole night long and the next day from morning until evening, but they could not find their way out of the forest.

At last they were so tired that their poor legs could carry them no farther. They laid themselves down under a tree and went to sleep. When they awoke, it was the third morning since they had left their father's house. They started out again, but it was no use. They only went still deeper into the forest, and they knew that if no help came soon they would starve.

The Wicked Witch

At last they saw a small house just a little way ahead of them. But how surprised they were when they came nearer to it. The house was built of gingerbread with sweetcakes and tarts stuck on the sides and roof. And the window was made of sugar.

"Oh!" exclaimed Hansel, "let us stop here and have a splendid feast. I will have a piece from the roof first, Gretel, and you can eat some of the sugar window."

Hansel reached up on tiptoe and broke
off a piece of gingerbread. He began eating
it with all his might, for he was very hungry. Gretel seated herself on the doorstep
and began munching away at the cakes of
which it was made. Suddenly, a voice came
out of the cottage.

    "Munching, crunching, munching,
      Who's eating up my house?"
Then the children answered,
      "The wind, the wind,
        It's only the wind."

The children went on eating as if they never meant to stop, not thinking that they might be doing something wrong. Hansel, who found that the cake on the roof tasted very good, broke off another piece. Gretel, who had taken out a whole pane of sugar from the window, sat down to eat it. Just then the door opened and a strange looking old woman came out leaning on a stick.

Hansel and Gretel were so frightened that they let fall what they held in their hands. The old woman shook her head at them, and said, "Ah, you dear children, who brought you here? Come in and stay with me for a while, and no harm shall happen to you." She seized them both by the hands as she spoke, and led them into the house.

For supper, she gave them plenty to eat and drink—milk and pancakes and sugar, apples, and nuts. When evening came, Hansel and Gretel were shown two beautiful beds with white curtains. They lay down in the beds and thought they were in heaven.

But though the old woman pretended to be friendly, she was a wicked witch. She had had her house built of gingerbread on purpose to catch children. She would feed them well until they were fat, and then cook them for dinner. This is what she planned to do with Hansel and Gretel.

Early the next morning the witch dragged Hansel out of bed and put him in a cage outside the house. She would feed him well and keep him there until he became fat. Then she would cook him for dinner.

The witch cooked a fine breakfast for Hansel. She gave Gretel only two crusts of bread. Every morning the old witch would

go out to the little cage and say, "Hansel, stick out your finger so I may feel if you are fat enough yet to eat." But Hansel knew the witch had weak eyes and could not see a thing so small as a finger. So he always stuck a bone, which she thought was his finger, through the bars of the cage. When she felt how thin it was, she wondered why he did not get fat.

Week after week went by and Hansel did not seem to get any fatter. After several weeks the witch got tired waiting. One morning she decided to eat Hansel for dinner that very day. But first she got the oven hot so she could bake some bread to eat, too. Then she dragged poor Gretel up to the oven door, under which the flames were burning fiercely. "Creep into the oven," she said, "and see if it is hot enough yet to bake bread." But if Gretel had done this, the witch would have shut the poor child in and baked her for dinner instead of Hansel.

Gretel guessed what she wanted to do, and said, "I don't know how to get in through the narrow door."

"Stupid goose!" said the old woman. "Why, the oven door is quite large enough for me. Just look, I could get in myself." As she spoke, she pretended to put her head in the oven.

Suddenly, Gretel thought of what she must do. She gave the old woman a big push that sent her right into the oven. Then Gretel shut the iron door and fastened the bolt.

Oh, how the old witch did howl! But Gretel ran to Hansel, opened the door of his cage, and cried, "Hansel, Hansel, we are free! The old witch is dead!"

Hansel rushed out of the cage. The children were so happy that they ran into each other's arms.

Now that there was nothing to be afraid of, they went back into the house and began looking around. In the old witch's room they saw an oak box which they opened. It was full of pearls and precious stones.

"These are better than pebbles," said Hansel, as he filled his pockets. "Now we are rich."

"I will carry some, too," said Gretel. Then she held out her apron. It held quite as much as Hansel's pockets.

Back Home at Last

"We will go now," said Hansel. "We must get away from this forest as fast as we can."

They walked for nearly two hours, and then they came to a big lake of blue water. "What shall we do now?" asked the boy. "We cannot get across, and there is no bridge."

"Oh, here comes a boat!" cried Gretel. But she was mistaken. It was only a white duck which came swimming toward the children. "Perhaps she will take us across if we ask her," said Gretel. Gretel began to sing, "Little duck, do help poor Hansel and Gretel. There is no bridge or boat. Will you let us sail across on your white back?"

The friendly duck came near the bank and Hansel sat down on its back. He

wanted to take his little sister on his lap, but she said, "No, we shall be too heavy for the kind duck. Let her take us over one at a time."

The good duck did as the children wished. She carried Gretel over first, and then came back for Hansel.

How happy the children were to find themselves in a part of the forest that they remembered quite well. As they walked on they saw more and more things they remembered, until at last they saw their father's house. Then they began to run and, bursting into the house, they threw themselves into their father's arms.

Poor man, he had been so very sad since his children had been left alone in the forest. He was full of joy at finding them safe and well again. "And now, my dear children," he was happy to tell them, "you have nothing more to fear. After you went away we had so little to eat that your stepmother would not live with me anymore. She went far away and I have not seen her since."

But how surprised the poor woodcutter was when Gretel opened her apron and shook the pearls and precious stones all over the floor. And he was surprised again when Hansel took handful after handful from his pockets. "Now we can be happy together," said the father.

Maggie and the Little Calf

Maggie Muggins ran as fast as she could to the cucumber patch to see Mr. McGarrity. Maggie had something on her mind, and that something was worrying her. Mr. McGarrity could see that, and he said to her, "Well, Maggie Muggins, what is troubling you this fine day?"

Maggie looked at him with eyes that were wide, and said, "It may be a fine day for you, Mr. McGarrity, and it may be a fine day for me, but I know someone who doesn't think it's a fine day."

Mr. McGarrity leaned on his red-handled hoe and looked sharply at Maggie. "Maggie," he said, "you don't mean to tell me that you know someone who isn't happy today?"

"Yes, Mr. McGarrity, I do. And to save my good two-M handkerchief, I don't know the because-why."

"But have you tried to find out, Maggie?" asked Mr. McGarrity.

"Yes, I have, sir, and all he does is cry. It's very sad, isn't it?" said Maggie.

"Well," said Mr. McGarrity, "maybe it is, and maybe it isn't. You see, I don't know who or what you are talking about."

A Little Calf Cries

"That's right, Mr. McGarrity, you don't. Well, I'll tell you," said Maggie. "I don't have any secrets from you, and anyway, this is not a secret. Anyone who goes down to the pasture can see him crying. Mr. Mc-Garrity, it's the little calf. He's standing down in the pasture all alone, crying his little heart out."

"Oh dear," said Mr. McGarrity, "that is sad."

"Yes," said Maggie. "And when I said to him, 'Little Calf, what's the matter?' do you know what he answered?"

"No," said Mr. McGarrity.

"Maa-a-a-a."

Mr. McGarrity laughed. "That wasn't very satisfactory, was it?"

"No," said Maggie. "So then I put it another way. I said, 'Little Calf, is there anything I can do for you?' and do you know what he said?"

"Maa-a-a?" said Mr. McGarrity.

"Yes," said Maggie. "That's all he said. And I'm worried, Mr. McGarrity."

"As well you might be," said the old gardener. "Maggie, wasn't there anyone around or about who might have told you what was the matter with him?"

Maggie shook her head. "There was no one but a little dog, away over by the fence. But he was laughing so hard, Mr. McGarrity, that I didn't go near him. I was feeling so sad for the crying little calf, that I thought if I went over to the laughing little dog, that I might laugh, too. And I wouldn't want to laugh when I am sorry for the little calf."

Mr. McGarrity's kind old eyes twinkled. "No, I don't suppose you would. But Maggie, just the same, the way I look at it is this way. The only thing to do is to ask the little dog why he's laughing. For all you know, the little dog's laughing may have something to do with the little calf's crying."

Maggie nodded her head. "Maybe you're right, Mr. McGarrity."

Mr. McGarrity nodded his head. "Yes, maybe I am. You see the whole thing is very mysterious. And in order to solve the mystery, we should use every possible clue."

Maggie agreed. "You're right again, Mr. McGarrity. I'll go question the little dog."

And Maggie left the cucumber patch, raced past the scarlet runners, under the hedge, across the south meadow and down to the pasture. She could see the sad little calf standing just where she had left him. She stood still for a little minute to listen, and she heard his soft sad "Maa-a-a." She sighed. Poor little calf! This was too fine a

day to be unhappy! She looked toward the line fence. The little dog was still there, and he was still laughing.

"Wow,wow,wow," he laughed.

Maggie went to him, and in her most polite manner said, "Hello, Little Dog."

Little Dog's answer was another burst of laughter.

Maggie raised her voice and said, "Little Dog, my name is Maggie Muggins, and I've come to ask you something."

Still laughing, the little dog said, "Go ahead and ask me, Maggie Muggins."

"Do you know why the little calf is sad?" asked Maggie.

"Ha ha ha . . . Yes, I do," laughed the little dog.

Maggie's red lips tightened, and she shook her finger at the little dog. "I'm surprised at you," she said. "I'm surprised that you'd sit there laughing when you know someone is sad."

"Oh, but it's so funny!" said the little dog. Tears of laughter were now trickling down his face.

"Well," said Maggie, "if it's that funny, I'd like to know about it. Will you tell me, please?"

Why the Little Dog Laughed

"Yes," said the little dog. "You know 'Hey, diddle, diddle'?"

"You mean,
'Hey, diddle, diddle, the cat and the fiddle,
The cow jumped over the moon;
The little dog laughed to see such sport,
And the dish ran away with the spoon.'"

"Yes," said the little dog. "That's the 'Hey, diddle, diddle' I mean. Well, I'm the little dog that laughed. I'm still laughing."

"You certainly are," said Maggie.

"And this time I can't stop laughing," said the little dog, "because this time the cow didn't get over the moon. She's caught up there. She's dangling in the sky."

Maggie Muggins couldn't speak. She was so surprised. The little dog went on with this story. He told her that the cow, who had been jumping over the moon for years and years, forgot that the moon changes.

She had always jumped over the moon when it was round like an O. "But last night," he said, "the moon was in her first quarter and shaped like a bow that shoots arrows. And when Mrs. Cow jumped over her, her horns caught on the hook of the moon. She's dangling up there and can't get down."

"And is she the sad little calf's mother?" asked Maggie.

"Yes, she is," said the little dog.

"Well, then," said Maggie, "no wonder the little calf is sad. Wouldn't you cry if your mother were dangling on the moon?"

"I haven't any mother," said the little dog, still laughing.

"Well, ask me if I'd cry if my mother were dangling on the moon," said Maggie.

"Maggie Muggins," said the little dog, "would you cry if your mother were dangling on the moon?"

"I certainly would," answered Maggie. "And you should be ashamed of yourself."

The little dog shrugged his shoulders. "I might as well laugh," he said. "Nothing can be done about it."

"There must be something," said Maggie. "And I know who'll know what to do. Mr. McGarrity! He knows everything. So I'm sure he'll know how to get a cow off the moon."

Maggie left the laughing little dog, and went back to the garden and Mr. McGarrity. He could tell by the way she was running that she had found out something. So he leaned again on his red-handled hoe.

"Oh, Mr. McGarrity!" Maggie cried when she came up to him. "That little laughing dog should be ashamed of himself. And do you know the because-why?"

"I'd never guess," said Mr. McGarrity.

"Well, you know 'Hey, diddle, diddle, the cat and the fiddle, the cow jumped over the moon; the little dog laughed . . .'?"

Mr. McGarrity dropped his red-handled hoe in surprise as he gasped, "Maggie, you don't mean the laughing dog by the fence is *that* little dog, do you?"

"Just what I mean, Mr. McGarrity," said Maggie, now dancing up and down in excitement. "He's the very little dog. And he's laughing because last night when the cow jumped over the moon, she got her horns caught on the hook of the moon, and she's stuck. Mr. McGarrity, she's dangling."

"No!"

"Yes. And that's why the little calf is crying. That cow that is dangling is the little calf's mother, Mr. McGarrity," said Maggie.

"No!"

"Yes, and Mr. McGarrity," went on Maggie, "we've got to get that cow down from the moon."

"But how, Maggie?" asked the old gardener.

"That, Mr. McGarrity, is up to you," said Maggie Muggins.

Rescued from the Moon

And it was then that Mr. McGarrity leaned on his red-handled hoe and began to think. It was not very long before he hit upon a plan. "Maggie," he said, "I think I have an idea. You have a big kite, haven't you?"

"Oh, yes," said Maggie.

"And it has a whole roll of cord on it, hasn't it?" asked Mr. McGarrity.

"Yes," said Maggie, "there are miles and miles of cord on it, so it can fly as far as the moon." Maggie's eyes brightened. "Why, Mr. McGarrity! That's what you mean, isn't it? You want my kite to fly to the moon."

"Yes, I do," said Mr. McGarrity. And he began to tell Maggie about his plan. He told her to take her kite out into the middle of the pasture. But before she let it go she must write a note on the tail of the kite to Mrs. Cow, to tell her what to do.

Maggie listened carefully to all Mr. Mc-Garrity had to say. Then she got the kite and wrote the note, which said:

Dear Mrs. Cow,

Fasten the tail of this kite

to your horns. We're going to

pull you off the moon.

Maggie Muggins

Maggie got the little laughing dog to help her hold the cord, because Maggie knew it was no easy thing to pull a cow off the moon. They let the kite go. They watched it go up, up, up. They saw Mrs. Cow putting on her spectacles to read the note.

They saw her fasten the tail of the kite to her horns. Then they saw her start her downward journey.

"She's coming, Little Dog, she's coming," cried Maggie Muggins. "Come on, Little Dog, run over to the fence. We don't want a cow to fall on us."

Mrs. Cow landed safely. She gave two or three breathless "moos" and looked around her. And the little calf was laughing.

That was all Maggie Muggins wanted to hear. "Little Dog," she said, "the little calf is laughing. I'm going back to Mr. McGarrity, and I'm going to tell him that you are a good little dog. You helped me get the cow off the moon."

Mr. McGarrity was very pleased with Maggie's good news. "The wind must have been just right," said Mr. McGarrity.

"Yes," said Maggie. "Everything was just right after we got started. The little dog helped me just right, and the cow tied the cord on her horns just right, and, Mr. McGarrity, I've never seen a happier cow and calf in all my Maggie–Muggins–days."

"And so must you be happy. You thought of the whole thing," said Mr. McGarrity.
"Oh, tra la la la la la loon!

We got the cow down from the moon! I don't know what I'll do tomorrow," said Maggie, as she skipped on down the garden walk.

Mr. Y and Mr. Z

Of all the storekeepers in town there are none so merry as Mr. Y and Mr. Z.

They have quite the grandest store on the street. Outside it is painted a bright, cheerful red, and inside it is full of all the things that a grocery store should have— soap and crackers and sardines and tubs of butter and red shiny apples. Besides, there are lots of shelves of everything you could possibly think of, all put up in cans.

Mr. Y is tall and thin, and Mr. Z is short and stout. Mr. Y has red hair, and Mr. Z has very little hair at all. Mr. Y can

reach all the things on the top shelves, and Mr. Z can get all the things on the bottom shelves. If there is anything on the very top shelf, they have to get a long pole and poke it down. Then Mr. Y pokes and Mr. Z catches, because Mr. Z's lap is the widest.

In fact, they do everything together. Mr. Y takes the money and Mr. Z rings the bell on the cash register. Mr. Y counts the groceries, and Mr. Z writes them down. Mr. Y makes the jokes, and Mr. Z laughs at them.

And, in the evenings, when the store is closed and work is done, then Mr. Y plays the flute and Mr. Z plays the accordion.

You would think that when two people get along so well together, they would never have a quarrel in the world. But once upon a time they did. This is how it happened.

For a long time they had been wondering what to do to make their life even merrier than it was. They had tried playing baseball with the soup cans and football with

the watermelons. They built all sorts of castles out of ketchup bottles and breakfast foods, just to see them come tumbling down again. But after a while they got tired of all this, and there just didn't seem to be anything new to play.

A Funny Idea

Then Mr. Y had a grand idea. He thought he would change the prices of everything in the store, overnight, just to see how surprised the customers would look when they came around next morning. He didn't want Mr. Z to know about it, so that it might be a nice surprise for him, too. For Mr. Y was always trying to think of something that would please Mr. Z.

But Mr. Z, too, was always trying to think of something that would please and surprise Mr. Y. And, unfortunately, he happened to think of exactly the same thing, and he thought of it at almost exactly the same moment as Mr. Y.

So each of them, very secretly, set about writing a whole set of new tickets. And each of them, also very secretly, went about sticking the new tickets just where they thought it would be most fun.

Mr. Y would turn his head suddenly and want to know what Mr. Z was giggling about, and Mr. Z would stop writing his

secret tickets long enough to ask *why* Mr.
Y was chuckling so. They would both go off
into peals of laughter and then look very
solemn and begin working away again faster
than ever.

Finally they locked up their store and
went home for the night.

The first customer to come next morning
was a housewife. She wanted three cakes of
soap for a quarter.

"Twelve cents apiece!" said Mr. Y, for he had changed the tickets from the breakfast cereal.

"But they're always three for a quarter," said the housewife.

"Not now, not now!" said Mr. Y. "Maybe you're thinking of soup. Soup's three for a quarter today," he added, and then began to giggle.

"Why, no, it isn't!" cried Mr. Z, beginning to giggle, too. "It's two for nineteen. Look at that!"

And he winked at Mr. Y, but for some reason Mr. Y didn't seem to think it was funny at all.

A Nightmare

"I tell you it's two for nineteen!" chanted Mr. Z, in an irritating sort of way, and he went about the store humming, "Two for nineteen, two for nineteen!"

"Just like a hen that's laid an egg!" thought Mr. Y. He began to get very annoyed, as people do when their jokes don't turn out to be funny after all.

The next customer wanted sugar and potatoes.

"Six pounds for fifteen!" shouted Mr. Z.

"Two for forty-nine!" yelled Mr. Y, banging his fist on the counter.

The customers began to get worried. They didn't know what to make of it all. And the more Mr. Y chuckled, the madder Mr. Z got, and every time Mr. Z giggled, Mr. Y was cross enough to bite his head off.

In the afternoon it was worse. No one knew what anything cost at all. Half the customers were buying all sorts of things they didn't need just because they were cheap, and the other half were shouting that they wanted their money back. As fast as Mr. Y stuck a ticket on one shelf, Mr. Z tore it down and put a different one in its place. They kept rushing around and around the store, doing nothing but changing the tickets.

The last straw was when Mr. Y marked a whole crate of watermelons four for fifteen cents. All the boys from the neighborhood came pouring into the store so fast one couldn't even count them. And above all the commotion, the customers snatching this and that thing—for by this time they were so confused that they started waiting on one another—you could hear Mr. Y's high, squeaky voice shouting, "Six for nineteen! Six for nineteen, I tell you!" and Mr. Z's deep bass rumbling, "Three for a quarter!"

It was like a nightmare!

When six o'clock came around, Mr. Y and Mr. Z were both exhausted. Mr. Y just rushed off down the street on his long, thin legs, looking neither to right nor left. Mr. Z shooed the last customer out of the store and then sank down on the onion crate and burst out sobbing.

He sobbed for quite a long time. When he had finished, he felt a little bit better. So he mopped his eyes and blew his nose. Then he jumped up off the onion crate and rushed out of the store, not even banging the door behind him, and pattered off along the sidewalk as fast as he could go.

It was the very first time in all their lives that Mr. Y and Mr. Z had not walked home together. For years they had hung their two little aprons up side by side at exactly six o'clock. At exactly two minutes past six they had taken their two hats and locked the store and strolled home side by side.

But this time Mr. Y hadn't even gone home at all. He was far too upset. He went striding along through the town very fast not caring at all which way he went, until he came to the place where the sidewalk ended and the country began. There Mr. Z finally saw him, still striding along with his nose in the air and his apron flapping like a flag in the breeze.

Friends Again

Now Mr. Y was walking much faster than Mr. Z, and so Mr. Z had to make his stout little legs work very hard indeed to catch up with him, but catch up he did. And as soon as Mr. Y heard that little patter-patter coming along behind him he slowed down a bit, and pretended to be looking at the landscape. So, side by side, but neither looking at the other, they went along the road and across a field, until they came to a big log that was lying under a hickory tree. There they both sat down side by side, just like that—plump!

Mr. Y was still very cross, and Mr. Z was still very hot and out of breath, so for a long while neither of them spoke. Then Mr. Y looked around at Mr. Z and gave a big sniff. And Mr. Z looked at Mr. Y, and he gave a sniff, too. And then they both began to wriggle and scuff their toes on the ground.

After a while Mr. Z said, "I shouldn't think you need be so mean, just because I did something I thought would please you!"

And Mr. Y said, "Well, you didn't have to be so cross, just because I wanted so badly to give you a big s-surprise!"

"I only did it to make you laugh!" said Mr. Z.

"I thought you'd be very pleased and m-merry!" said Mr. Y.

Then Mr. Y pulled a packet of lemon drops out of his apron pocket.

"Have one," he said to Mr. Z.

Mr. Z took one and sucked it, and then he pulled a little packet out of his apron pocket, and he said to Mr. Y, "Don't you want some chewing gum?"

Half an hour later, just as the sun was setting, anyone looking out of his front window might have seen two figures. One was very tall and thin and the other was very short and stout. They were trudging along together, arm in arm.

They were Mr. Y and Mr. Z, going back to their grocery store. And from what I hear, they have never quarreled since.

Greased Lightning

Zeke Has a Friend

Zeke went down to the pigpen to look at his beautiful, muddy little rascal of a playmate. After a while he climbed over the fence and began to scratch the pig's back. If Greased Lightning had been a cat he would have purred.

Out of his overalls pocket Zeke took two oatmeal cookies his mother had given him—big, fat, delicious cookies. He gave one to Greased Lightning and began eating the other one himself. The pig ate his in two noisy gulps and tried to snatch Zeke's cookie as well.

"Such manners!" Zeke said, giving the pig half of his own cookie. "You're acting like a pig." And then he started to laugh. "That's funny—" Zeke said, "a pig acting like a pig."

91

"Greased Lightning" by Sterling North. Copyright 1940 by Holt, Rinehart and Winston, Inc. Adapted and reprinted by permission of Holt, Rinehart and Winston, Inc.

He laughed until he was tired. Then he lay down beside Greased Lightning and looked up at the windy clouds scampering like a litter of white pigs across the blue sky overhead.

To tell the truth, Greased Lightning knew perfectly well that he was a bad little pig. How he skedaddled out of the garden when Zeke's mother came to pick peas!

"Eeeee . . . Eeeee . . . Eeeee!"

Like a flash of pink lightning, he would streak down the bean rows. And usually he could find the hole in the fence a split second before Zeke's mother could give him a rap with the tin dishpan she always brought to the garden.

"If that scalawag ruins my little yellow tomatoes, that'll be the end of Greased Lightning," she would tell herself. "Pop can't get along for a week without yellow tomato preserves."

Safe beyond the fence, the little pig would already be thinking up new mischief. He really wanted to be good. But always the sun was so bright, and the wind was so warm, and the world was so beautiful on the other side of the fence. It made him sure, made him feel in his bones, made him absolutely know that he was going to be a bad pig again.

First he would run back and forth looking for a hole. Then he would root under the bottom wire and lift. Finally, one way or another, he would slip through the fence. And, once outside, he would kick up his heels and scamper like a colt. He would run through the grass like a young bull calf.

"I'm out again . . . I'm out again . . . I'm out again," he would squeal, and his little pig heart would be as full of joy as a wild strawberry is full of sweetness.

One sunny morning, Zeke was swinging his legs thoughtfully as he sat on the fence looking down at Greased Lightning. What a fat, saucy, little rascal he was! No wonder he was always getting himself into trouble. Now if Lightning could only do something brave and daring, he might turn out to be a real hero.

Zeke giggled at the idea of Greased Lightning being a hero. "But," he thought, "if Lightning would save my life or something, Pop would have to let me keep him."

Then, out loud, he said to the pig, wallowing happily in the mud, "Oh, Lightning, if you can't be good, why can't you be brave? And if you can't be brave, why can't you be good?"

"Oink," said Greased Lightning.

"All you seem to think about is getting through the fences—"

"Oink," said Lightning.

"—and stealing Mom's garden stuff and spoiling her yellow tomatoes. You're always up to something."

The little pig felt ashamed. He didn't say a thing, and he wouldn't look Zeke in the eye. He began to snap at the yellow butterflies dancing like flakes of sunlight on the mud around him. He looked very gay for a pig that was being scolded.

"You'd better turn over a new leaf," Zeke said. "You'd better start being good, or save my life or something."

A Wonderful Secret

Greased Lightning didn't know what "turn over a new leaf" meant. He thought it

95

meant to turn over a new oak leaf and find
another acorn. He started to smile, a wide
pig smile because he had a wonderful secret,
and the secret was this—

By getting through only two fences, he
could reach a beautiful woods on a nearby
farm. And there under the oak trees were
bushels of last year's acorns. Some of the
acorns were wormy, of course, and some of
them had sprouted. But there were enough
with good white meats to make a small pig
think that he had found a free soda foun-
tain where they give away double chocolate
sundaes.

But free ice cream or free acorns! Look
out! There must be a catch in it somewhere. And sure enough, Zeke and Greased

Lightning found the catch the very next morning.

When the sun arose, Greased Lightning, as usual, was missing. And when Zeke finally found the pig, he was in the neighbor's oak woods, turning over old leaves and greedily eating nice bitter acorns.

Zeke had completely forgotten the fierce dog that guarded the farm—a dog he feared although he would not admit it. The pig didn't want to go home, and the boy loved the smell of the oak leaves and the cool shade. So they wandered under the trees, startling squirrels and rabbits. They poked their noses into hollow logs and stopped to drink at a cool spring.

They were very happy until they heard a
deep growl and the rush of padded feet on
the oak leaves. Zeke and Greased Lightning
jumped up and ran like deer for the far

fence and safety. Up one path and down
another they fled, with the big dog gaining
on them. They could hear the great beast
panting behind them. Zeke was afraid that
they would never make the fence.

Zeke caught his overalls, struggling over the fence. So at that very moment, Greased Lightning turned on the dog, lowered his head, stiffened his front legs, and squealed in rage. The dog was so startled he skidded to a stop. This gave Zeke just enough time to get free from the barbed wire and over the fence.

A moment later Greased Lightning came dashing through a hole too small for the dog. And there they were, safe on their own farm!

Once, in a storm, Zeke had saved Greased Lightning. And now Greased Lightning had saved Zeke. But, alas, he could not tell the story at home. Pop would laugh at Zeke for being afraid of the dog.

It was not as if Greased Lightning had saved the boy from a wolf or a rattlesnake. The whole countryside would have praised the pig for such a deed. But it was a fine thing the pig had done. Now, more than ever, they were friends.

Greased Lightning Goes to Market

All through the month of June, Zeke was careful not to say anything about the pig. It was like some dangerous game that Zeke must play exactly right so that no harm could come to Greased Lightning.

Only once again did Zeke's father threaten to eat the little pig. That was when Greased Lightning foolishly rooted up all the yellow tomato plants. On these grew the pear-shaped yellow tomatoes that Zeke's mother made into such wonderful preserves.

But Zeke wasn't really worried until one morning when his father came out of the milk house, shouting, "Who dumped that crock of cream?"

100

There, not twenty feet away, was Greased Lightning, grinning from ear to ear, his face smeared with cream right up to his eyes. He was so full of cream he could hardly waddle, and he was so pleased with himself he was nearly laughing out loud.

"That settles it," said Zeke's father. "That pig's going to market . . . Zeke, Zeke, come here! Lock Lightning up in the pigpen."

Zeke knew that there was no use pleading for his friend. When his father talked like that, Zeke knew he meant it. Cream was precious at Zeke's farm. And now Greased Lightning had spilled a great crock

101

of the stuff, all that had been skimmed from the morning and evening milkings of the day before. No words could move Zeke's father.

Zeke's father and mother thought that Zeke would quickly forget. It wasn't as if he were losing a dog or a pony. Greased Lightning was only a pig—and not a very good pig at that.

But after they had gone to bed, Mother did say, "You might fix your fences, Eb, so pigs could not get through them."

Eb turned over and pretended that he was asleep.

But Eb couldn't face his son and he knew it. He got up just before dawn, loaded Greased Lightning into a crate, piled the baskets of produce around him in the wagon, and hitched up the team of bays.

Zeke awoke to hear the jangle of the wagon. He knew exactly what was happening. His father was taking Greased Lightning to market.

He jumped out of bed, hurriedly washed himself, combed his hair, and put on clean overalls.

Then he tiptoed down the steep back stairway. He stopped long enough in the pantry to get a brown paper sack full of bread and oatmeal cookies. Soon the boy was saddling his pony, making ready to follow his father.

All the way to Cherry Valley, Zeke was never more than a mile behind. The boy cut across pastures and wood lots that he knew. Hidden by hedges and haystacks, he followed as closely as he dared without letting his father see him.

Greased Lightning, riding backward in his crate, looked out over the tailboard of the wagon. Lightning wasn't very happy. Riding backward made him sick. And the scenery had a funny way of rushing away from him as though he were sliding downhill tail first.

It was market day. The courthouse square of Cherry Valley was a-buzz with excitement by nine o'clock that morning. Chickens clucked and ducks quacked.

More than one hundred dogs were howling, fighting, yelping and barking, sniffing and snapping, because this was the day of the great dog auction.

Village housewives with their market baskets on their arms were already moving from wagon to wagon. They pried and punched and pinched the fruit, making really green melons so soft that later customers thought they were ripe.

Yes, half the country was there to buy and sell, to dicker and dawdle. And Eb had his wagon parked at the very best corner. A hand-lettered sign on the pig crate said,

FOR SALE, CHEAP!

ORNERY PIG!

GOOD BACON!

People stopped to look at the pig and to talk to Eb. But no one really wanted to buy. It wasn't the time of year to kill pigs in the first place. It was too hot to work, and too hot to eat pork.

Zeke tied his pony in the shade of a big maple tree on one of the back streets. He then made his way carefully to the crowded square. All day long the boy lay in the dust under the flowering bushes near the court-house, hidden from view by the green leaves. Once in a while he ate a piece of bread or munched slowly on an oatmeal cookie.

Every time someone stopped to talk to his father or to look at the pig, he clenched his fists tightly and whispered, "Please, don't buy my pig."

106

A Greased Pig Race

Late in the afternoon a man came along who seemed really interested. He was a big, fat, ugly-looking man dressed in a bright blue suit and a derby hat. He poked at Greased Lightning with his cane and blew smoke rings in the pig's face from his big, black cigar.

The fat man was saying, "Bacon! I don't want him for bacon. I want him for the greased pig race."

"Greased pig race? What greased pig race?" Zeke's father asked.

"Tomorrow's the Fourth of July," said the fat man. "It will be the greatest Fourth ever. There will be free lemonade, fireworks, parade, band concert! And there will be many fine games. One of them is the greased pig race. All we need is a pig. I'll ask the committee. Chances are we'll buy him."

Long before breakfast the next day, Cherry Valley was in an uproar. First there was the parade led by the band in bright blue uniforms, with brass horns gleaming. Then came two companies of war veterans with a drummer and an American flag.

Next came the mayor in the town's only automobile. And small boys on decorated bicycles shouted loudly above the blare of the band.

Following the mayor were all the fancy floats drawn by horses whose manes were

109

entwined with red, white, and blue ribbons. The girls on the floats wore white dresses with red sashes and blue hair ribbons. They squealed when firecrackers went off too near them.

It was all a wonderful sight. If Zeke hadn't been worrying about his pig, it would have been the biggest day of his life.

But now the fat man came puffing through the crowd to buy Greased Lightning. He reached in his pocket for his money and handed Zeke's father a ten-dollar bill.

"No, no, no," Zeke whispered, his heart beating wildly. But he knew that nothing he could do would stop the sale of the pig.

About ten o'clock the three-legged races, the horseshoe pitching, and the pie-eating contests began. And then came the awful moment.

"Greased pig contest!" shouted the fat man.

"Oh, boy! oh, boy!" screamed all the young boys.

"His name's Greased Lightning," shouted the fat man. "Fastest, slipperiest hog ever seen in these parts."

"Let us at 'im!" screeched the excited boys.

Zeke Saves His Friend

But Zeke, now crawling out from beneath the bandstand, thought his heart would stop beating. He saw his beloved pig, his own Greased Lightning, dragged from his crate. Rough hands smeared him with great lumps

of lard. He heard his frightened squeals and
saw his useless struggles.

Then, torn between fear and joy, Zeke
prepared for the battle. He hitched up his
pants, retied his shoelaces, and rubbed his
hands in the dirt. He spat on the ground
and drew a circle around it for good luck.

In the mob of boys lined up for the race, all somewhat dirty and nine-to-twelvish in age, any boy named Zeke might have passed unnoticed even by his own father. There were so many pie-smeared faces and bright, eager eyes. So many pairs of brown legs and brown arms looking almost alike.

The boys were breathing hard and jostling and elbowing for the best positions. They were whistling between their fingers and making catcalls. Zeke wondered if he could ever outrun some of the bigger boys who seemed almost six feet tall. What chance did he have against a mob like this? His spirits sank.

Two big tears welled up in the corners of his eyes, and he brushed them away fiercely with his clenched and dirty fists.

"The boy who catches this pig can keep him," the fat man was saying. "Isn't that right, Eb?"

"I got my ten dollars," Eb said. "It's not my pig. But that's the rule. The boy who can catch that pig can keep him. A bargain's a bargain."

A moment later, at a shot from the starter's gun, they were off. Whee! Around the courthouse they raced, over the beds of lilies, under the Civil War cannon, and over the neat pile of cannon balls, into the barberry bushes and out again. There were torn shirts, scratched elbows—and then as they went through a lawn sprayer—loud shrieks as the cold water doused them.

Whoops! Over went a baby buggy—luckily an empty one. There went the banana cart, scattering yellow fruit among the screaming spectators. Half a hundred boys raced on.

At first the bigger boys were way ahead of Zeke. His mouth got hot and dry and his

side hurt. But he pumped away as fast as his legs would carry him around and around and around the courthouse after his pig.

Once a big, red-headed boy had Greased Lightning in his arms. But the pig was so frightened (and so slippery) that at last he broke away and all the youngster had was a thick coating of lard.

People were shouting and laughing until they cried, but Zeke and Greased Lightning were running and fighting for their very lives.

And then Zeke had a bright idea. If he could cut behind that clump of lilac bushes and head the pig off! And now, with a burst of speed, he was within ten feet of Lightning. Zeke made a flying tackle—and hung on just as tight as he could.

"Lightnin', Lightnin', Lightnin'," he sobbed. And Lightning, hearing Zeke's voice, gave a squeal of joy and stopped struggling. He snuggled close to Zeke, nuzzling him.

116

Sssss—BOOM—ahhhhhh! A sky rocket sizzled up into the evening sky. A very tired boy and a very tired pig were sitting in Eb's wagon watching the fireworks display. Pinwheels, sparklers, red fire, and Roman candles flashed in the darkness.

"Oh, Pop! Look at that one!" shouted Zeke. He squeezed his greasy pig in excitement. And a very tired pig was thinking to himself, "Now I'll be the best pig in the world. I certainly will. And I'll never, never, never . . . well, hardly ever . . ."

He had heard Zeke's father say, "A bargain's a bargain, son."

And then he heard Zeke say, "Maybe I can help mend your fences, Pop."

And Zeke's father had said, "I'll need all the help I can get, son. Looks like we're going to have that pig around for the rest of our lives."

The Owl and the Pussy-Cat

The Owl and the Pussy-Cat went to sea
  In a beautiful pea-green boat,
They took some honey, and plenty of
    money
  Wrapped up in a five-pound note.
The Owl looked up to the stars above,
  And sang to a small guitar,
"O lovely Pussy, O Pussy, my love,
  What a beautiful Pussy you are,
            You are,
            You are!
  What a beautiful Pussy you are!"

Pussy said to the Owl, "You elegant fowl,
  How charmingly sweet you sing!
Oh! let us be married, too long we have
    tarried:
  But what shall we do for a ring?"

118

They sailed away, for a year and a day,
  To the land where the Bong-tree grows;
And there in a wood a Piggy-wig stood,
  With a ring at the end of his nose,
        His nose,
        His nose,
  With a ring at the end of his nose.

"Dear Pig, are you willing to sell for one
    shilling
  Your ring?" Said the Piggy, "I will."
So they took it away, and were married
    next day
  By the Turkey who lives on the hill.
They dined on mince and slices of quince,
  Which they ate with a runcible spoon;
And hand in hand, on the edge of the sand,
  They danced by the light of the moon,
        The moon,
        The moon,
  They danced by the light of the moon.

—Edward Lear

How Doth the Little Crocodile

How doth the little crocodile
  Improve his shining tail,
And pour the waters of the Nile
  On every golden scale!

How cheerfully he seems to grin
  How neatly spreads his claws,
And welcomes little fishes in
  With gently smiling jaws!

—Lewis Carroll

PART 3

Tales of Interesting People

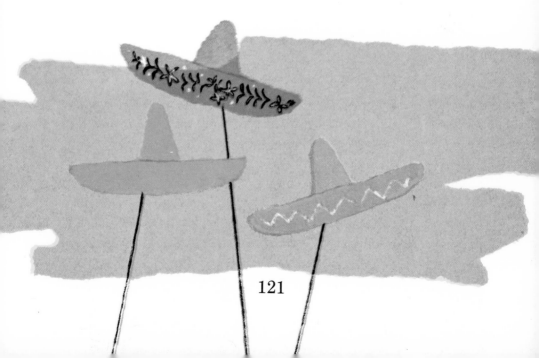

Beto and His Many Sombreros

Beto is a little Mexican boy who lives with his father and mother in the country of Mexico. Mexico is south of the United States, and it is warm there most of the time. Beto does not live in one of the big cities. His home is on a farm near a small village.

The houses in this part of the country are made of brick. Before the people could

122

build their homes, they had to make the brick. This was done by shaping wet mud into square blocks and drying them in the sun. Houses made of these mud bricks are called adobe houses.

The men and boys who work on the farms like to wear bright-colored clothes. Their coats are not like the coats we wear. They are colorful blankets that have a hole in the middle so they can be slipped on over the head. Then part of the blanket hangs down the back and part of it hangs down the front. They call this kind of a coat a sarape.

But, even though the Mexican farmer may be poor and cannot buy very good clothes to wear, he likes to have a good hat. His hat has a very wide brim and stands up high on top of his head. It is called a sombrero.

Beto Wants a New Sombrero

For many months Beto had wanted a new sombrero. Every day he thought about what kind he would like to have. For one thing, it would be black with many bright colors embroidered on it. It would have a wide brim with little balls that dangled and bounced at the edge, and a cord that tied under his chin.

When he told his mother about his wish, she said, "You already have many sombreros, little Beto. Why do you want another?" But even as she said this, she turned her head away and smiled, since she already knew why.

"This one would be for the fiesta," Beto said. "For the first time in my life I am going to the fiesta with you and Papa. When I dance at the fiesta I would like to have a very gay sombrero. I want one that ties under my chin so it will not fly off when I bounce up and down."

Papa was listening as he sat at the table eating tortillas and beans for breakfast. (Tortillas are pancakes made of ground corn. Many Mexicans eat tortillas and red beans for breakfast, lunch, and dinner.)

"Little boys must earn new sombreros," he said.

"But, Papa, how can I earn a new sombrero?" asked Beto eagerly.

"In a family, when a boy does his work well, perhaps he can earn his wish. Who knows?" said Papa. "But now it is time for a boy called Beto to feed the chickens and turkeys and gather the eggs. The eggs must be sold at the market today."

Beto sighed and walked over to the wall where several sombreros hung. He took down an old straw one and put it on his head. It was torn in places and a bit ragged at the edges. When he leaned over to scatter the feed in the yard, a hen took a peck at the tatters, thinking it was something to eat!

Beto found so many chicken and turkey eggs that he had to carry them in his sombrero to the house, making three trips.

"This sombrero is good for carrying eggs, but it will never do to wear at the fiesta," Beto told his mother. "It is too old."

"That is so," his mother said. "But perhaps even a little old sombrero may help to find the way to a little boy's wish. Who knows?"

After breakfast it was time for Beto to hitch up the little gray burro and go to market with the eggs.

"My little sombrero with the wide red band around it is the one I will wear to market," said Beto. He hung up the old straw one and took down a small, bright-colored one.

Papa helped him put the eggs in baskets on the little burro's sides. Then Beto jumped on the burro's back.

"Get a fine price for the eggs, and see that you remember to buy all the things your mother told you to get," said Papa. "And do not be slow about getting back in time for lunch. *Adios.*"

After Beto had sold the eggs in the market, he remembered to buy the limes and other fruit and also some new dinner plates for his mother. He packed all these things in the baskets and then used his last penny to buy a piece of candy. He wanted very much to visit the booth where the sombreros were sold, but it was getting late. So

127

he rode back home, wearing his small, bright-colored sombrero.

"This is a fine sombrero for going to market," he told his mother, "but it is too small to wear to a fiesta."

"That is so," his mother said. "But perhaps even a very small sombrero may help to find the way to a little boy's wish. Who knows?"

Mama was glad to have Beto home in time for lunch. She served tortillas and beans on the plates, and fruit with lime juice for dessert.

After Beto had all the food he could eat, Mama said, "The sun is very hot, Beto. It is time now to take a siesta."

So Beto put on his biggest sombrero and went outside to take a siesta under a palm tree.

Ah, but it was shady and cool under the big sombrero!

"This is a fine sombrero for siestas," said Beto to his mother when he woke up. "But it is much too big to wear to a fiesta. It would bump into all the dancers and knock them down."

"That is so," said his mother. "But perhaps even a very big sombrero may help to find the way to a little boy's wish. Who knows?"

Beto Thinks Fast

After a supper of tortillas and beans, Papa said, "Your mother and I are going down the road to take some eggs to our neighbors. You must stay home and see that the coyotes do not carry off our chickens and turkeys, little Beto. Take good care of them. *Adios*."

Beto sat down by the door watching his parents go down the road with the basket of eggs. The sun was sinking low in the sky, and the chickens and turkeys were flying up in the trees and bushes to roost for the night. It was quiet and peaceful all around.

129

It wasn't quiet for long. In the distance Beto heard the barking of a band of coyotes coming nearer. The chickens and turkeys stirred uneasily.

"What shall I do?" thought Beto. As he bent over to pick up a big stick, suddenly Beto had an idea. He ran to the wall in the house where the sombreros hung. Quickly he gathered them all in his arms and put one in each window of the house. He put the tallest one on his head, and began to walk back and forth in front of the windows with the big stick over his shoulder.

Louder and louder screamed the coyotes. Closer and closer they came. Faster and faster beat Beto's heart.

"What if the coyotes carry off the hens and turkeys?" Beto worried. "Then there will be no eggs to sell. I will not earn a new sombrero if I do not do my work well."

The coyotes crawled in very close to the chickens and turkeys. They snarled and showed their teeth as they barked and looked up into the trees. Beto trembled with fright. Any minute now he thought the fierce animals would rush in to grab his chickens and turkeys.

All at once the snarling coyotes began to move back toward where they had been hiding. Suddenly the evening was quiet. Beto kept on walking by the windows, but he could see the band of coyotes standing still as they looked toward the house.

"Aha," said Beto. "Maybe I have them tricked. They think there is a person under each sombrero at the windows. They think that I am a very tall man with a gun."

Sure enough, suddenly the coyotes turned and ran down the road as fast as they could.

Beto Gets a New Sombrero

Just then, Beto's father and mother came home.

"Beto! Beto!" they called. "Did the coyotes come and gobble up all of our chickens and turkeys? We heard them making a terrible racket, but we could not get here any faster."

Papa and Mama were smiling as they heard the story Beto told. "My sombreros helped me feed the chickens, gather the

eggs, ride to market, and take siestas," Beto told them. "And now they have helped me in another way. All the coyotes were scared and ran away because of my many sombreros."

"Very good," said Papa, beaming at Beto. "But now you will need still another sombrero, one that will help you dance at the fiesta. Tomorrow we shall go to the marketplace. We will sell some eggs and one or two of the chickens and turkeys that you saved from the coyotes. Perhaps there will be enough money to buy the very sombrero you want. Who knows?"

Mama smiled at Beto. "That is so," she said. "Your many sombreros have helped you to find the way to your wish."

And that is how Beto danced at the fiesta wearing a black sombrero with many colors embroidered on it. It was just the kind he had always wanted, with little balls that dangled at the edges and a cord that tied under his chin so it wouldn't fly off when he bounced up and down.

A Tulip for the Queen

Dirk Goes to Holland

When Dirk Riggs was ten years old, he went to Holland to visit his Uncle Dirk Vandermere. It was spring and almost tulip time.

On the trip over, Dirk thought of the wonderful sights he would see—windmills, sailboats, dog carts, dikes, and canals. Best of all, on the Queen's birthday, he might see the Royal Tulip Parade. On this day the Dutch children carried tulips to the palace steps as a birthday gift to the Queen.

Holland is a very interesting country. It is called The Netherlands in other parts of the world. Netherlands means "lowlands." Part of Holland is lower than the sea. Many years ago these lowlands were covered with water. But the people built banks of dirt to keep the water out so that they could grow things on the land. These dirt banks are called dikes. The dikes are several feet thick and often have roads on top of them.

135

Many people in Holland wear the same
kind of clothes that people wear in America; but some of them still wear the old
Dutch clothes like their grandparents wore.
These clothes are made of wool and most
of them are black. The men's and boys'
trousers are wide and are sometimes called
pantaloons. They wear wooden shoes. Many
of the women and girls wear black, wide
dresses with striped aprons and white
peaked caps. They also wear wooden shoes.

In Holland there are many farms. The farmers grow vegetables and grain. They also have cows and from the milk they make very good cheese. It is sold all over the world.

The Dutch people also make dishes and vases of clay. And they have large flower gardens. Holland tulips are very beautiful. Tulip bulbs, too, are sold all over the world.

When Dirk arrived in Holland, nothing was as he had dreamed it would be. Cold fog hid the country. Not a tulip or a dog cart was in sight.

137

He was met by his Uncle Dirk, who was dressed like an American. Dirk and his uncle bowed and shook hands with each other. But Dirk could not speak the language of the Dutch people and his uncle could not speak English; so they could not say anything to each other.

Uncle Dirk lived in a brick house beside a canal. Behind the house there were seven greenhouses where Uncle Dirk grew thousands of tulips. In front of the house was a boat landing where two boats were tied—a cabin motorboat named the "Van Vliet" and an old sailboat named the "Black Swan." The "Black Swan" was not used anymore because it was too slow.

Uncle Dirk raised tomatoes and tulips and shipped them by water to all of Holland and to other countries in Europe. The tomatoes made him rich, but the tulips made him proud. Every year, Uncle Dirk's tulips had won a prize ribbon at the Keukenhof Fair.

As the days passed, Dirk was not quite happy. He was very proud of being named for his uncle and wanted to please him, but how could he ask questions when he could not speak Dutch?

In his heart, Dirk wanted three things. He wanted his uncle to be proud of him, he wanted to ride on the "Black Swan," and to see the Royal Tulip Parade.

At last, the day of the trip to Keukenhof arrived. Dirk awoke early and looked out of his window. As usual, it was dark and foggy. He dressed and hurried downstairs.

In the kitchen, Uncle Dirk was standing by a window, looking out at the sky. He greeted Dirk with a smile and motioned for him to sit down to breakfast.

After a breakfast of cheese, bread and butter, and cocoa, Dirk and his uncle each

put on wooden shoes and a jacket, and
started for the boat landing. It was so foggy
outside that they could see nothing except
the two lights that showed where the boat
landing was.

On the way, they were met by Will and
Pete, the two gardeners, who were pushing a
cart with a little glass house on top. Inside
were Uncle Dirk's prize tulips that he was
taking to the Keukenhof Fair.

Uncle Dirk and the gardeners talked excitedly. Pete explained in jerky English that the tulips must not get cold, for they must bloom at just the right time for the Fair. That is why they were carried in a glass house. A door in the glass room was opened and quickly shut again. Dirk saw that the tulips were just budding. By the time they would arrive at the Fair these buds would be in full bloom.

Dirk followed his uncle onto the motorboat and they shoved off.

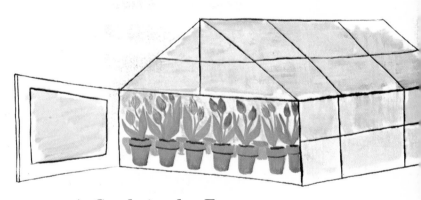

A Crash in the Fog

As the "Van Vliet" glided down the canal, Dirk tried to see the land, but the fog was like gray fur before his eyes. Dirk shivered. The cabin was closed, but the air inside it was cold and damp. Would such cold air ruin the tulips? Dirk pulled his jacket tighter and sat watching his uncle.

Uncle Dirk was studying the tulips. He was very worried about them. He raised his hand to open the glass door just a little when a loud CRASH! sounded behind them. The "Van Vliet" lurched—her engine sputtered—then stopped. Dirk bounded out of the cabin to see what had happened!

In the fog, another canal boat had crashed into the "Van Vliet," damaged one end of it badly, and splintered its rudder.

Dirk ran back into the cabin. There sat Uncle Dirk bandaging his hand that had been cut by the shattering glass. Close beside him lay the broken remains of the glass house roof. Inside the broken house, no longer protected from the cold and fog, stood the tulips. How could they win at the Fair if they got cold and damp?

Dirk got up all his courage. Motioning with his hands, he asked Uncle Dirk if he could go for help.

Uncle Dirk did not know how to say "yes" in English, but he nodded his head up and down, which meant the same thing.

Dirk lost no time, for already he was thinking of a plan, a plan that he thought would work, if only there was enough time!

He peeled off his muffler and laid it over the hole above the tulips, then paddled to the shore of the canal on a rubber raft. When he reached the canal road, he started on foot, back toward Uncle Dirk's house.

The fog was no better. Dirk ran and ran. When he could go no farther, he sat down on a little bridge to rest. He was about to start up the road again when a dim light shone through the fog. He could hear the clap-clap of horses' hoofs. As though from nowhere, a pony, pulling a cart of milk cans, and a driver came into view.

Dirk gave a wild wave with his handkerchief and asked if he might ride. The driver motioned Dirk to a seat beside him and off they trotted. It was nearly twenty minutes before the two lights at Uncle Dirk's boat landing gleamed before them.

A Ride on the "Black Swan"

Dirk thanked the driver, then ran to the greenhouse to look for Will and Pete. Pete understood what must be done. They untied the "Black Swan" and sailed away!

At last Dirk was having a ride on the "Black Swan"! How smoothly she glided, how gracefully she skimmed along.

Pete looked at his watch, then at the sky. He got out a map to show Dirk. From the map, Dirk could see that it was quite a long way to Keukenhof. Could they get there in time for the Fair?

Soon the wind blew stronger and stronger. This made the boat go faster and faster. In a short time they came to the "Van Vliet." The glass flower house was moved onto the "Black Swan" and they continued on their way to Keukenhof. The wind rose higher and higher. Pete began to worry whether such a strong wind might break the old sails on their boat. Suddenly, there was a loud ripping sound. Dirk looked up and saw that the main-sail of the "Black Swan" had ripped in two! Everything seemed lost!

Dirk Gets to the Fair in Time

But Pete noticed that they were very near a large lake and in the lake was a big boat going toward Keukenhof. Pete asked the captain if he and his friends could ride to the Fair on his boat.

"Come aboard, and welcome," said the captain.

That night, the boat reached Keukenhof. Dirk slept in a house that was owned by a friend of his uncle. His room was strange but cheery.

The next morning, when Dirk awoke, the sun was shining brightly. On the table beside his bed was a newspaper, printed in English. When he saw the front page, he could hardly believe his eyes.

It was the Queen's birthday! There was her picture. She had come to Keukenhof to see the Flower Fair and was staying at the Royal Town Palace.

Outside, Dirk had never seen such flowers before! Red, pink, purple, yellow, orange, white, and some were almost black. Dog carts full of hundreds of flowers passed by.

At the end of the garden walk was a big gray-colored tent. Here, the tulip growers showed their very best tulips. Winners got prize ribbons for their flowers.

148

When Dirk came to the place where his
uncle was to show his flowers, he looked
around to see what prize ribbon his Uncle
Dirk had won this year. But there was no
ribbon at all! Then Dirk understood why.

Inside the glass house where the tulips
should have been blooming in all their
beauty, there was only *one* in bloom. The
cold had kept the other buds from opening.

Dirk looked sadly at the one lonely flower. Then his sadness began to leave him. It was a kind of tulip different from any he had ever seen. It was a blue color! Blue as the sky on the brightest day.

The people were being seated now. The speaker asked for quiet. Then he read the names of all of the people who had won prizes for their flowers. Dirk wished his uncle's name was one of them, but it was not. Finally the prizes were all given out. Dirk thought his uncle looked disappointed.

Dirk Leads the Tulip Parade

Then came a surprise! The speaker announced that he was about to give a prize for the most unusual tulip at the Fair. In a clear voice, he said, "The Royal Medal will be given for a flower, chosen this day by the Queen, to be planted in the Royal Palace Gardens."

A hush fell over the great crowd of people; then they heard the name of "Dirk Vandermere" called out.

Uncle Dirk rose and went forward. A gold medal on a ribbon was placed around his neck.

Dirk was excited and filled with joy to see his uncle receive such an important

151

prize. Then, imagine how surprised he was to hear his own name called out: "Dirk Riggs."

Slowly, Dirk went forward.

The speaker said, first in Dutch and then in English, "Because your acts of bravery brought this flower to Keukenhof, it is the wish of the Queen that the tulip be given the name 'Sword of Courage.'"

Uncle Dirk cut the lone blue tulip and presented it to Dirk. Holding it high, Dirk led the Royal Tulip Parade to the Palace of the Queen.

Curiosity

Nobody ever seems to mind
When my dog is trying to find
What's inside of a rubber ball,
Or what's in back of a garden wall;
Or goes to the kitchen just to see
What dessert is going to be;
Or runs to see, when the doorbell's ringing,
What the delivery boy is bringing.
But everyone keeps telling me
To stop my curiosity.

—Monroe Stearns

New Friends

Yesterday I was a stranger at school.
When the principal sent me to my
  new room,
I was greeted by a sea of wide, curious
  eyes, and silent, unmoving lips.
My friends were left behind.

But today is a happy day because my
  new friends
are waiting with smiles and friendly chatter
to walk with me to school.

PART 4

Tales of Early America

An Indian Thanksgiving Gift

Timothy Brewster strode along whistling and swinging a small wooden bucket. His brown eyes searched for walnut trees as he neared the woods by the river. Mother wanted nutmeats for the Thanksgiving stuffing she planned to make.

Timothy's family had come to the southern part of Kansas in early spring, and Father had especially chosen a place close to the river, where there would be trees.

Some of the settlers on the same wagon train with the Brewster family had stopped in Nebraska. Others had gone on west or into the Oklahoma territory. But Father said, "I want to live where there are trees so we can build a log cabin. A home without trees around would never seem right." And Timothy was glad they did have trees nearby as he thought of how good the walnuts were going to taste in the turkey stuffing.

It was a long way to the walnut trees, so Timothy had taken along slabs of cold cornbread, sweetened with wild honey, for a lunch. As he walked along now, he felt a crisp, cool breeze against his cheeks. The autumn sky seemed bluer than in spring, and the trees blazed with vivid shades of red and yellow.

"It's fun to look for nuts," thought Timothy, "but I wish I could have gone with Father." His father had started for the settlement, several days' travel away, to sell a wagon-load of corn and to get supplies. He had hoped to be back before Thanksgiving, which was only a few days off.

Yes, riding on the wagon with Father would have been fun. "If I had a pony to ride, it would be even more fun," Timothy said to himself. "But money for horses is scarce. Father could only afford the price of the one team and wagon. Still, I would like to have a pony!"

For a moment, Timothy daydreamed of himself flying over the countryside on a beautiful spotted pony.

Timothy Helps an Indian

Timothy rounded a bend in the faint trail he was following and stopped suddenly. All daydreaming fled with the terror he felt. His heart froze with fear. There, a short distance ahead of him, lay an Indian.

Timothy's hair felt as if it were standing straight on end, and his legs felt weak and wobbly. He had heard frightening stories about what some Indians had done to settlers.

Timothy wished he could run away. But he was afraid to move for fear the Indian would see him. As he stood rooted to the spot, Timothy began to realize the Indian had not moved once. Then he heard the Indian give a low, faint moan. Cautiously, Timothy backed away a few steps and turned to run. Then he stopped.

"If the Indian is hurt, is it right to run away and leave him?" Timothy asked himself. "He is a person just as I am. Father says you should always help someone who is in trouble, no matter who it is."

Slowly Timothy retraced his steps and crept up to the Indian and stared down at him. Now Timothy could see that the Indian was in great pain. One leg lay twisted strangely. The Indian had a broken leg.

Timothy went to the nearby river and brought water in the little wooden bucket. He bathed the Indian's face, which was hot and dry to his touch. Slowly the Indian's head moved, and he opened his eyes to stare coldly at Timothy. Timothy offered him water and helped the Indian to drink.

There was a look of thankfulness in the proud, dark eyes when Timothy gave the Indian the lunch he had brought along for himself. The man ate like a wolf, gulping the food as if he hadn't eaten for days.

"What to do now?" Timothy wondered. He couldn't carry the Indian, and he didn't want just to leave him lying there. Slowly the Indian sat up, then pulled a long, sharp knife from his belt. Timothy stumbled backward.

"Is this the way the Indian is going to thank me for helping him? By trying to stab me?" thought Timothy in horror.

But the Indian pulled off his shirt and began cutting, to tear it into strips. He pointed to Timothy, then pointed to a tree nearby and back to himself.

"He wants me to get tree limbs to make splints for his broken leg," cried Timothy. Realizing the Indian had meant him no harm, Timothy nodded and hurried to get the straightest willow limbs he could find.

Stripping off the leaves and small branches, Timothy carried several back to the Indian, who cut them in lengths, wincing from the pain of his leg as he worked.

The Indian slowly and painfully straightened the twisted leg. Timothy heard a small snap as the bone was set back in place.

161

The Indian gritted his teeth and turned pale. But he did not cry out, for Indians were taught from childhood to be brave.

With Timothy's help the splints were laid along the leg and tightly bound into place, holding the leg stiff.

"How will he walk?" Timothy wondered after the leg was set.

As if reading his thoughts, the Indian pointed to a forked young tree nearby and handed the knife to Timothy.

"He wants me to cut it for a crutch," said Timothy and did as the Indian wished.

With the aid of the forked stick, the Indian slowly pulled himself to a standing position, as Timothy helped him up. Then,

giving the sign of friendship, the Indian began hobbling away. From time to time he turned to look at Timothy. Just before he disappeared from sight, Timothy smiled and waved good-by. The Indian returned the wave and was gone.

Father Returns

Timothy stood staring after him a moment. Then noticing the time of day, he hurried on to the walnut trees to fill his wooden bucket with nuts for his mother.

"I don't believe I will tell Mother now about the Indian," thought Timothy. "With Father away, she would only worry about an Indian being so close to home. When Father comes back, I'll tell them both about the Indian."

Two days later, Timothy heard the sound of wagon wheels and horses' hoofs along the trail. He ran to a tall cottonwood tree and climbed up. Far off he could see his father's team and wagon coming over a hill.

"Mother! Father's coming!" shouted Timothy. Sliding down as fast as he could, he

163

ran to meet his father, while Mother waited inside the doorway to welcome him.

"How wonderful to have you home," smiled Mother. "We've missed you so. We've worried each night for your safety."

"See all the things he bought!" cried Timothy.

Timothy was so very full of excitement over his father's return and the many things in the wagon that the story of the Indian was forgotten. For, among other things, there was corn meal, a length of cloth for Mother's new dress, and a shirt and pair of overalls each for Timothy and his father. There was also a bag of dried apples and a sack of expensive white flour.

"We truly have much to be thankful for on Thanksgiving," sighed Mother, her face beaming over all the nice things.

Brave Eagle Visits Timothy

The next day was Thanksgiving, and Mother was up early, preparing dried apple pie, pumpkin pie, loaves of white bread, and baked squash. As Mother worked, Father told her of some troubles people had had farther west with the Indians.

Some white hunters had broken the peace treaty and had hunted on the Indian's land. In great anger the Indians had burned one of the settler's houses.

"If the soldiers don't catch those hunters, and if they come into this territory, they may cause trouble with the Kickapoo Indians. And their chief, Brave Eagle, can be terribly fierce when he wants to be," said Father.

Hearing Father tell about the Indians reminded Timothy of his Indian with the broken leg. He just started to tell about it when he heard a thunder of horses' hoofs.

Running to the window, he stared out. "Look!" Timothy cried out. "Indians! A big band of them are just coming over the hill."

Mother gasped, "What shall we do?"

Now Father stared out at the approaching band a moment, then said, "Nothing. They don't have on war paint. It looks as if they have come for a visit." Father went to the door and stood waiting. Timothy peered around one side of his father.

"It is Brave Eagle, the Kickapoo Chief," whispered Father as the Indians drew near.

"That's the Indian I helped," thought Timothy, staring at the big Indian. "How different he looks now. He isn't dirty or

166

muddy. What a beautiful necklace he is wearing."

Brave Eagle pulled up short and made a sign of peace. One Indian drew up beside him and began speaking broken English.

"Brave Eagle, mighty chief of the Kickapoo, comes in peace. He comes—bring gift to his friend, Little Red Hair."

Father turned around to stare in puzzled astonishment at Timothy.

Timothy moved forward and made the peace sign to Brave Eagle, who returned the sign.

"But what does he mean?" Father asked Timothy.

A Reward for Timothy

Before Timothy could answer his father, the other Indian began speaking again. "Brave Eagle hurt. Horse step in gopher hole and fall. Throw Brave Eagle off. Break leg. Horse run off—leave Brave Eagle far away from home. Little Red Hair find Brave Eagle. He kind and help. Brave Eagle remembers—brings gift for his friend."

Then another Indian rode forward leading a beautiful pinto pony. Brave Eagle
took the lead rope, handed it to Timothy,
and made the sign for friend.

"Brave Eagle will always be Little Red
Hair's friend," spoke out the Indian who
knew English.

"Oh, thank you so much!" cried Timothy,
his face alight with happiness.

Though Brave Eagle didn't understand the English words, he could tell by Timothy's face how he felt.

And then, nodding his head, Brave Eagle waved good-by with his hand, as he recalled Timothy doing to him. Then he turned his horse and rode away in a cloud of dust, followed by the other Indians.

After the Indians were gone, Timothy told his father and mother about Brave Eagle and what had happened.

"That was the right thing to do," said Father.

"—and a brave thing to do. Bless you, dear," said Mother, giving Timothy a hug.

"It will do much to help us and other settlers keep the peace—doing such a kindness for the Indians," said Father.

Timothy patted the spotted pony and whispered another thank you for the wonderful gift. He was glad to have a friend like Brave Eagle, and glad there would be peace with the Indians.

"We truly do have much to be thankful for," said Timothy.

A Visit from the Indians

The day before New Year's, 1859, young Tom Cabot and his nine-year-old sister, Becky, were outside their clapboard house with its log cabin kitchen, trying out their new snowshoes. They were newcomers in the Ontonagon country of Michigan, having settled in the wilderness with their parents the summer before. Each day they became more fond of their home, but knew little of the history and customs of the country.

Tom bent to tighten the deerhide thongs on his snowshoes and, when he straightened up, was quite surprised to see shadowy forms coming from the woods toward the

170

Plank Road. Up until the heavy snows came, this road had been a busy highway. All day long heavily-laden ore wagons, pulled by patient oxen, creaked by on their way to Copper Harbor. There, boats came to carry "the red dust," as miners called it, across the lake. Now, in the heavy silence of winter, with snowdrifts taller than a man, the Cabots hardly ever saw anyone.

Tom finally found his voice, "Indians!"

Brother and sister, startled, watched the figures breaking trail through the tall pine trees.

"I wonder what they want," said Tom.

"I can't imagine," said Becky. She knew that in warm weather the Chippewas harvested wild rice in the nearby marshes.

Occasionally, she saw several men on the edge of the forest in the summer. But she had never seen so many at one time.

"Perhaps they're hunting," she said.

"I don't think so," said Tom. "Maybe they need help. I think we should tell Mother."

Gifts for the Indians

Mrs. Cabot had also seen the men from the window and wondered why so many had gathered near the settlement. She was not concerned because she knew that the Chippewas lived peacefully with their neighbors.

Tom ran into the house and pointed out the window. "Tell me," he asked his mother, "why are so many Indians gathering at one time?"

"I don't know. That has me puzzled, too," said Mother.

Becky spoke up. "Maybe Mrs. Boyd could tell us." She was their nearest neighbor, a half mile away, and they hadn't seen her since the snowstorm. It was after Christmas, when her husband, another miner, had returned to work with their father.

"Let's find out." Tom was eager to go. Soon three pairs of snowshoes went crinch-crunching down the hill.

Their neighbor saw them coming and opened her door with a cheery "Come in, come in!" The house had a sweet, tantalizing smell. "You're just in time for some fresh bread. I'm sure I can spare one loaf from the batch I made for the Indians."

"For the Indians!" Even Mrs. Cabot couldn't conceal her surprise, and the black

brows above Tom's dark eyes were question marks of disbelief.

"You don't mean you're giving this good bread to them? Any kind of bread, old and stale, would be plenty good enough for them."

"I certainly am," Mrs. Boyd spoke sharply and her quick glance at Tom made him feel rather uncomfortable. "Why Tom," she said, "they are our neighbors," and this land was theirs long before we settled here. We've built our cabins on their hunting grounds and I feel honored to share some of our food with them. We look forward to their visit every year."

She turned to Mrs. Cabot. "Perhaps you don't know, but it is the custom of the Indians hereabouts to visit their white neighbors on New Year's Day. You'll probably have visitors, too, tomorrow."

"Well, I declare!" said her neighbor, genuinely interested. "So that's why so many went by this morning. I'm glad to know."

Mrs. Cabot paused now and her eyes narrowed as she thought of all her cupboard

174

supplies. The children's father had brought home stock for their winter needs from the company store when he was home for Christmas. "What would the Indians like? What can we make for a treat?"

"I know what," said Becky, thinking about her favorite sweet. "Let's make gingerbread cookies for them." And her eyes danced at the thought of tomorrow's visitors. Mrs. Boyd had no children at all. Maybe there would be some girls her own age. Even though they couldn't understand one another, it would be fun just meeting.

Her mother spoke slowly, looking at Mrs. Boyd. "I do have plenty of flour and molasses and ginger."

"I think ginger cookies would be a fine treat. Of course, it will be quite a job making cookies for two or three dozen people."

"Will there be that many?" asked Tom.

"Maybe more, maybe less. You never know," said Mrs. Boyd.

Tom swallowed the last of his third slice of the golden bread. It was rich with raisins and the flavor lingered pleasantly on his tongue. "What else will there be?" he wanted to know.

"Oh, just everything. Some make doughnuts, some pastries. The storekeeper hands out plenty of tobacco for the men and women, and sometimes pickled herring or a few slices of salt pork. And the children, of course, get rock candy."

"Whew! I'd sure like to be an Indian on New Year's Day!" said Tom. His words led everyone to laughing. Then he went on. "Just suppose you didn't give them anything. What then?"

"They wouldn't do any harm, if that's what you mean," said Mrs. Boyd, putting aside any ideas he might have about a fight. "They'd probably wait around the house until they got tired, then go away." She added, "It seems to me anyone could spare something for the Indians once a year."

"After taking their lands and so much from them, it is a mighty small return.

Sharing makes for good neighbors, and small kindnesses are not often forgotten."

The Cabots Make Cookies

All afternoon Mrs. Cabot made cookies, with Becky helping to cut them out and put them in the pan with the pancake turner. Tom, more interested in the preparations for the visitors than he cared to show, kept the woodbox filled up and the fire going.

It was dark and candles had to be lighted before the last batch of dough was out of the oven. With the last of the dough, Becky had cut out a gingerbread man for Tom, and a gingerbread girl for herself. Finally, the cookies had cooled and were packed in a box.

Here Come the Indians

Next morning Mrs. Cabot decided to mix more cookie dough. It wouldn't hurt to be prepared. Tom and Becky could hardly wait for their guests to come. They kept looking out the window to see if any were coming and whooped with delight when they saw some twenty or more plowing through the snow toward their house.

There were several boys and girls, and there were women with babies on their backs. There were men wrapped in blankets to keep out the cold and snow.

None of the newcomers made any effort
to come to the door. Instead, when all had
arrived, they faced each other in a circle,
and slowly started stamping in the snow.
They kept up a continuous chant that
sounded to Becky like "How-wow-wow-in-
ish-a-shin, how-wow-wow-in-ish-a-shin."

"What do you suppose it means?" Becky
whispered to her brother.

"I don't know, but I wish I did," said
Tommy.

Their mother now carried a huge pan full of cookies to the open door and asked the visitors to come inside. Immediately the stamping and chanting stopped, but they made no effort to come any closer.

A very old man, who seemed to be the leader, finally approached. He took a cookie

and slowly bit into it. Then he swallowed another bite, and another, until the whole cookie had disappeared, evidently to his entire satisfaction.

Meanwhile, the three Cabots stood anxiously near. What if he didn't like their treat? But they needn't have worried. He licked his lips in evident enjoyment, again nodded his approval, took the pan of cookies offered to him, and passed them around to his own people.

Tom and Becky watched the Indians eat the cookies and remembered their own special cookies. Becky brought them from the cupboard, never dreaming what a sensation they would cause.

Before you could say "Jack Robinson," their visitors became aware that their cookies were shaped differently. The boys and girls, especially, looked at their cookies, then pointed to Tom's and Becky's.

The Indian children were unhappy. Some threw their cookies in the snow, although a moment before they had been enjoying them.

The Cabot children were so astonished at their reaction, they didn't take a single bite. The old man came back and held out his hand. Becky gave her gingerbread girl up instantly. After all, as Mrs. Boyd said, the Indians were their guests, and guests should be welcome to the best treats they had to offer. Besides there were plenty of round cookies and they all tasted the same.

Tom didn't give up his gingerbread man so easily. He broke his cookie in half, crammed the lower part into his mouth and gave the older Indian the other half. The old man gave Tom a look that was both sad and disturbed as he took the piece of cookie.

After a brief discussion, the leader was back. He held up a round cookie and shook his head from side to side. Then, holding up what remained of the special cookies, he nodded his head several times up and down.

"Well!" said Mrs. Cabot. "The Indians do not want round cookies. They would rather have the ones that are shaped like boys and girls." But after all, there was more dough and maybe . . . . Suddenly she had an idea.

An Indian Artist

She went to the group and touched three of the women on the shoulder and motioned for them to follow her into the house. They made no move, but looked at their men, and to her surprise, three men followed her instead. "Well, we'll see," she said grimly to herself, and put the breadboard on the table and started rolling out the dough.

She took a knife and marked out a gingerbread boy, then handed the blade to the

nearest man, and pointed to the dough. He grinned, and in no time had cut out a fish, an eagle, and a bear.

He seemed to be enjoying himself immensely, as his hand flew up and down the board.

"Look!" said Tom, "he's an artist!"

Becky lifted the dough into the long black pan and put it into the oven. And as soon as the cookies were baked and cooled, they were quickly sampled. One by

one the rest of the tribe had entered the room silently and Mrs. Cabot added coffee to the kettle of water on the stove. For the children she had raspberry jelly, which she had made from the wild berries in July.

Indians Always Remember

Their New Year's Day party turned out to be a great success. Long before dark their guests took leave. Their actions, if not their words, were understood.

"If that Indian," said Tom, referring to the Indian who cut out the cookies, "had had any buttons on his clothes, he would have burst them off, he was that proud of himself."

"He had reason to be," his mother replied. "He is a fine artist."

185

"I think they all enjoyed the cooking lesson almost as much as the food," Becky said.

"All I can say," Tom summed it up, "is it's a good thing New Year's Day comes only once a year." His arms were tired from carrying wood.

The Cabots saw no Indians for several weeks. And then one day the elderly leader of the tribe appeared at the door. He handed a quart of maple syrup to Mrs. Cabot and a package to each of the children. Tom was a little surprised to find that his maple sugar canoe was only half the size of Becky's.

But, on second thought, Tom knew that he deserved it. He had learned his lesson. Next time he would share all that he had when neighbors came to visit.

186

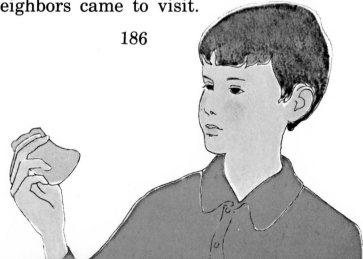

The Wolves of Lone Valley

When Sarah was twelve years old, she lived in a mountain cabin with her parents and her three brothers, who were named Bill, Josh, and Dave. Bill and Josh were younger than Sarah, and they were her playmates, after the daily chores were done on the little ranch. But Dave was seventeen, and he worked most of the time with his father, taking care of the animals, building corrals, and mending fences. Dave had helped cut the tall pine trees that made the log cabin, and he had laid the heavy stone floor in the big main room.

Winters in Lone Valley, where they lived, were long and cold. One morning in January, when clouds hung over the pine trees, Sarah's father spoke to the family very seriously. "I am taking the wagon and team to Beaver Crossing to get hay and grain for the animals," he said. "The sky looks as if we're in for a blizzard, and if we get snowed in for the rest of the winter, there isn't enough feed left for the animals."

"How long will the trip take?" asked the children's mother.

"I should be back by dark," the father replied. "But if I'm right about a storm coming, we should get ready in other ways besides getting in feed."

"What you can do, son, is to hike up the valley to Gant Withers' place and borrow two of his bear traps. I saw bear tracks up behind the corral this morning, so we may be able to lay in some meat."

Sarah and Bill and Josh looked at one another. They were all thinking the same thing: maybe they could go with Dave! The Withers family lived a mile up the valley, near a waterfall that fell into a wide, round pool. The children knew that the pond

188

would be frozen at this time of year in a smooth sheet of ice.

Father took a long rifle from the gun rack and said good-by as he walked out of the cabin and climbed into the wagon. The three younger children watched as he drove away, then turned to Dave in excitement. "May we go to the Withers' with you?" they begged.

"You aren't old enough," said Dave, teasingly. "I can walk faster if I go alone."

"I'm six years old!" said Bill.

"I'm ten!" yelled Josh.

"And I'm twelve!" put in Sarah. "I'll soon be thirteen!"

Dave smiled. It was always like this. Whenever the children wanted to go with him, trapping or hunting or walking the fence-line, they always called out their ages just as though that made them bigger and stronger. Actually, Dave enjoyed having them with him, and he usually gave in after teasing them.

"All right," he said now. "If Mother says you can go, it's all right with me."

The younger children looked at Mother, who was beginning to clear the breakfast table. "Yes, you may go," she said, "but first you must bring in wood, and make your beds, and clean up the bedrooms."

A Hike up the Valley

Sarah and Bill and Josh flew to the tasks, and when the chores were done the children began pulling on their boots, and coats, and woolen scarves, hoods, and mittens.

Dave was ready and waiting, so they soon started through the valley. The snow was crunchy underfoot, and the air felt cold and sharp to their noses. The dark clouds were

thick on the mountains, and as the hikers walked along together, they kicked a wide path in the snow. When they came to the rock slide at the bend in the valley they stopped and looked up at the huge stone resting on its edge, high overhead. It was

called Dead Chief Rock because against the sky, it looked like the face of an Indian with his eyes closed.

"He's got a chunk of snow on his nose!" laughed Bill.

"How, Chief!" yelled Josh, cupping his hands around his mouth. Usually, when they called to the Chief, an echo bounced back from the mountain, and it seemed as though he called back. But the clouds were low and heavy today, and there was no echo. Even Josh's voice sounded soft and muffled.

191

Not long after they left Dead Chief Rock they came in sight of Gant Withers' cabin, nestled among the tall pine trees close to the mountainside. As they drew nearer, the three Withers children ran from behind the cabin and dashed through the snow to greet them. Then Mrs. Withers came to the cabin door, waving, and Gant walked over from the barn.

Dave went to greet the grown-ups, but the six young children all raced for the frozen pool beneath the waterfall. What a

wonderful time they had! They slid down the slope by the pond and out across the slick ice. They built a snow tower and crashed through it laughing and tumbling over one another.

Time for Lunch

At noon, Mrs. Withers called them all into the cabin for lunch, and they took off their wet wraps and hung them before the fire so the things would dry while they ate.

Gant Withers sat at the head of the table. He was a big man, with black bushy whiskers and a loud booming voice. "So your pa found bear tracks down by your place, eh?" Gant roared. "Well, I can tell you why that bear is down out of the high mountains—it's because of the wolves!"

"We've seen them!" said Tom Withers.

"They howl at night!" put in Jane.

"There are hundreds of them!" shouted Kitty.

"Hold on!" boomed Gant. "It isn't that bad! But those wolves are hard pressed for food, and they're coming down out of the mountains. They're chasing all the game ahead of them. That's why Mr. Bear is down by your place. He's trying to get away!"

"Have you tried trapping the wolves?" Dave asked.

"Yes, I have," replied Gant Withers. "I've got traps up on the ridge, back of the barn, but so far they've been too smart to take the bait. They walk all around the traps, and I see tracks, but the bait is too cold for them. They'll leap at anything warm, with a fresh odor, and tear it to pieces. But you can't fool a wolf with cold bait!"

When lunch was over, Mrs. Withers went over to feel the line of clothing that was drying by the fire.

"These things are ready," she announced to the children. "You'd better get ready and start home. The clouds are lower, and it could start snowing any time now. It's going to blizzard tonight, for sure."

Sarah and Josh and Bill pulled on their warm trousers and buttoned up their coats, and wound the scarves around their chins and pulled their caps down over their heads.

194

"That's a mighty fine coat, Josh," said
Mrs. Withers, running her hand over the
boy's shoulder.

"Mother made it," said Josh proudly. "It
used to belong to Old Rocky."

Old Rocky had been a big sheep, and
when he died from eating poison weed,
Josh's father had skinned him, and his
mother had made the heavy pelt into a
coat. The smooth skin was on the outside,
and the wool inside. It was bulky, but was
the warmest coat Josh had ever had.

Josh Sees a Wolf

Now, with many good-by yells, Dave and the three younger children stomped into the narrow valley. It was easier walking on the way home, for they were going downhill, and the two iron bear traps they had borrowed clinked at Dave's side, where he had fastened them with a leather strap.

The misty snow clouds were drifting like smoke through the valley, and the air was damp. Once in a while the children could feel a sharp, cold sting on their faces, and they knew it would not be long before a bad snowstorm would begin.

As they rounded the bend in the valley, Josh looked up to laugh again at the snow on the nose of Dead Chief Rock, but

instead of laughing he stopped and grabbed Dave by the arm. "Look!" he gasped. "Look on top of the rock!"

The others stood still and looked up. There on the ledge behind the Chief crouched a long, gray animal! While they watched, he turned silently and disappeared behind the rocks.

"It was a wolf!" whispered Bill, without moving.

Dave grabbed Bill's hand and gave Sarah and Josh a rough push. "Start running!" he ordered. They ran by Dead Chief Rock now, and into the clearing beyond. Sarah looked back over her shoulder and saw the wolf, below Dead Chief Rock now, pacing back and forth along the ledge.

"Keep running!" Dave called to the younger children.

"I can't run any farther," gasped Bill, stumbling along.

"Sarah, put your arm under Bill's on that side," said Dave. "I'll grab him here, and we'll carry him along. Just keep your feet going, Bill!"

Chased by Wolves

Back across the valley, now, there came a deep-throated howl, followed by a series of sharp, quick yelps. The wolves were following them!

Suddenly, Dave thought of what Gant Withers had said: *They'll leap at anything warm, with a fresh odor.* "Josh!" yelled the older brother. "Throw off your scarf. Throw it off!"

Josh tore the scarf from around his neck and threw it into the snow. In just a minute, the yelping behind them turned to snarls and growls as two wolves reached the warm scarf and tore it to shreds.

"Your coat, Josh!" panted Dave. "Throw your coat!"

Josh's cold hands struggled with the big buttons on his heavy coat and loosened them. Then he wriggled out of it, still running. The coat dropped to the snow, as the girl and her brothers raced on.

Down the valley they could see their own cabin now, but behind them the wolves were still yelping. There were three of the wolves in front, and another farther back, racing to join them. As the big gray creatures reached the sheepskin coat, their yelps changed again to snarls and growls as they yanked the tough pelt through the

snow, ripping it apart and biting into the warm wool.

The cabin was just across the clearing now, and as they ran toward it the door flew open. Dave saw their mother stand for a moment, peering out into the gray light. Then suddenly she disappeared. An instant later she came from the cabin again, with Dave's rifle in her hand. Just as the four running figures reached the cabin door, she took careful aim, and fired.

The sound was short and dull in the heavy air, but out in the clearing one of the wolves fell in the snow. At once the other wolves pounced on their fallen companion, tearing him with their powerful jaws.

Sarah and Dave and Josh now pulled their mother into the cabin, and then Dave threw the heavy wooden bar across the door. They stood in the center of the main room, listening to the battle of the wolves in the clearing. There were more of the animals now, drawn from the mountains by the sound of the chase through the valley.

Josh threw two heavy logs on the fire, then he and Mother helped Sarah and Bill out of their wraps.

"You sure shot straight," Dave said to Mother, with an admiring smile.

"It wasn't hard," she said modestly. "The wolf was a good target against the snow."

Before long, the yelps and howls died away, and there was silence. Then Dave lifted the wooden bar and opened the door. A great swirl of snow flew into the cabin,

like millions of tiny beads of ice. "The blizzard has started!" Dave shouted.

Father Returns

Just then a faint call came from somewhere out in the blizzard. "Hal-ooooo!" It was their father.

Dave grabbed his coat, and a lamp from the table, and stepped out into the clearing.

Soon they heard the creaking of the wagon wheels, and heard the horses snorting impatiently. "Here I am, Dave!" shouted their father, who was very near but hidden by the curtain of snow. "Come and help me take this load to the barn. The horses have been feeling their way for the last mile, and I thought we were lost. Is everything all right?"

"Sure!" yelled Dave. "We're fine!" Then he turned to look at his mother and the younger children, and they all laughed!

The Big Bear

How the Brents Lived

Many years ago, when Indiana was a very young state, great forests of tall trees and tangled underbrush darkened what are now bright fields and sunny hills. On the bank of Big Blue River, a mile or two north of the point where that stream crosses the Michigan road, stood a cozy log cabin of two rooms—one in the front and one in back. The back room was a kitchen, and the front room was the bedroom, sitting room, and library all in one.

The house faced the west. Stretching off toward the river for a distance equal to twice the width of an ordinary street, was a blue-grass lawn. On the lawn stood a dozen or more elm and sycamore trees, with a few honey locust trees scattered here and there. At the water's edge was a deep slope of ten or twelve feet. Back of the house, mile upon mile, stretched the deep, dark forest, inhabited by deer and bears, wolves and wildcats, squirrels and birds.

203

"The Big Bear" adapted from THE BEARS OF BLUE RIVER by Charles Major with permission of The Macmillan Company.

In the river there were so many fish that they seemed to invite the boys to catch them. There were bass and black suckers, sunfish and catfish, and the sweetest of all, the big-mouthed redeye.

South of the house stood a log barn, with room in it for three horses and two cows. Surrounding the barn and five or six acres of land, was a fence eight or ten feet high, made by driving poles into the ground close together.

In this enclosure the farmer kept his horses and cows, a few sheep, and some chickens, geese, and ducks. The fence kept the wild animals out at night.

The name of the man who owned this farm was Balser Brent. Mr. Brent and his young wife had moved to Blue River from North Carolina when their small boy, Little Balser, was five years old. They had bought this eighty acres of land from the United States for one dollar an acre. President James Monroe had signed the bill of sale.

When this story happened, Little Balser was thirteen or fourteen years old. He had a younger brother, Jim, aged nine, and a little sister, one year old.

On the south side of the front room was a fireplace. The chimney was built of sticks, thickly covered with dried mud. The fireplace was very large. It was broad and deep enough to hold logs that were so large they could not be lifted. They were rolled across the floor and into the fireplace.

The father usually kept two extra logs, one on each side of the fireplace, ready to be rolled in as the blaze died down. The children would sit on these logs at night and do their arithmetic lessons on a rough slate made from a flat stone. The fire usually furnished all the light they had, for candles were expensive in those days and the family only used them when they had visitors.

The fire gave enough light. Its glare on a cold night went halfway up the chimney and sent a cozy glow to every nook and corner of the room.

The back room was the storehouse as well as the kitchen. From the beams along the wall hung rich hams and bacon, deer meat, dried apples, onions, and other provisions for the winter. There was a glorious fireplace in this room also, with an iron bar above it that swung in and out so pots could be hung on it for cooking food.

The floor of the front room was made of logs split in halves with the flat side up. The floor of the kitchen was just dirt, packed hard and smooth.

The farmers in those days had no stoves. They did their cooking in round pots called Dutch ovens. They roasted their meats on a spit or steel bar. The spit turned in front of the fire until the meat was cooked. Turning the spit was the children's work.

South of the fence that enclosed the barn was the clearing—twenty or thirty acres of land from which Mr. Brent had cut and burned the trees. On this clearing the stumps still stood but the hard-working farmer planted seeds between and around them. Each year he raised enough wheat

207

and corn to feed his family and his animals. He usually had enough left to take to Brookville, sixty miles away, where he would trade it for some things they needed that could not be grown on the farm or found in the forest.

The daily food of the family all came from the farm, the forest, or the river. They made their sugar from the sap of the sugar maple trees; their meat came from pigs they raised and from animals that lived in the woods. In the forest there were deer, bears, squirrels, rabbits, wild turkeys and pheasants. There were so many of them that a few hours of hunting would supply the table for several days. And there were many fish in the river. They were easy to catch.

Balser Goes Fishing

One day Mrs. Brent took down the dinner horn and blew two loud blasts upon it. This was the signal that Little Balser, who was working in the clearing with his father, should come to the house. Balser was glad to drop his hoe and to run home.

When he reached the house, his mother said, "Balser, go down to the river and catch some fish for dinner. Your father is tired of eating deer meat three times a day, and I know he would like a nice dish of fried fish at noon."

"All right, Mother," said Balser. And he immediately took down his fishing pole and line, and got the shovel to dig bait.

When he had dug up some worms, his mother called to him, "You had better take a gun. You may meet a bear. Your father loaded the gun this morning, and you must be careful in handling it."

Balser took the gun, which was a heavy rifle considerably longer than himself, and started down to a bend in the river, about a quarter of a mile away.

There had been rain during the night and the ground near the river bank was soft. Here, Little Balser noticed fresh bear tracks, and his breath began to come quickly. He looked closely into every dark bush, and looked behind all the large trees and logs. He had his eyes wide open all the time. He didn't want Mr. Bear to step out and surprise him with a friendly hug and put an end to Little Balser forever.

He walked on very carefully, somewhat tremblingly, until he reached the spot where he wanted to fish.

Balser was not very big, but his father had taught him how to use a gun. Although he had never killed a bear, he had shot several deer. Once he had killed a wildcat, "almost as big as a cow," he said.

No doubt the wildcat did seem "almost as big as a cow" to Balser when he killed it, for it must have frightened him greatly. Wildcats were always dangerous animals. Balser had never met a bear face to face and alone. But he thought, and many times had said, that there wasn't a bear in the world big enough to frighten him, if he had a gun in his hands.

He had often imagined and even carefully described to his parents and little brother just what he would do if he should meet a bear. He would wait calmly and quietly until the bear would come within a few yards of him, and then he would slowly lift his gun. Bang! And Mr. Bear would be dead with a bullet in his heart.

But when he saw the fresh bear tracks, he began to realize that he would probably have an opportunity to put his ideas on how to kill a bear into practice. He began to wonder if, after all, he might become frightened and miss his aim.

Then he thought of how the bear would be calm and would put his own ideas into practice by walking very politely up to him, and making a fine dinner of a certain boy whom he could name.

But as Balser walked on and on and no bear appeared, his courage grew stronger. As the possibility of meeting the enemy grew less, he again began saying to himself that no bear could frighten him. He said over and over that he had his gun and he could and would kill the bear.

A Bear Surprises Balser

So Balser reached the place where he wanted to fish. After looking carefully around him, he leaned his gun against a tree and carefully unwound his fishing line from the pole. Then he walked out to the

end of a log, which reached out into the river about twenty or thirty feet.

Here he threw his line into the water. Soon he was catching so many sunfish and bass that all thoughts of the bear went out of his mind.

After he had caught more than enough fish for dinner, he thought it was time to go home. As he turned toward the shore, imagine, if you can, what a chilling surprise it was to see upon the bank, quietly watching him, a huge brown bear.

If the wildcat had seemed as large as a cow to Balser, how big do you suppose the bear looked to him? As big as a cow? An elephant, surely, was small compared with

the huge brown fellow standing upon the bank. At least, Balser thought so.

It is true that Balser had never seen an elephant, but his father had, and so had his friend, Tom Fox, who lived down the river. They had agreed that an elephant was "just about as big as all outdoors." That was how big the bear looked to Balser.

The bear had a contented look about him that seemed to say, "That boy can't get away. He's out on the log where the water is deep. If he jumps into the river I can easily jump in after him and catch him before he can swim a dozen strokes. He'll have to come off the log sooner or later, and then I'll proceed to have him for dinner."

214

About the same ideas had been passing through Balser's mind. His gun was on the bank where he had left it, and in order to reach it he would have to pass the bear.

He must not jump into the water, for any attempt to escape on his part would bring the bear upon him instantly. He was very frightened but cool-headed for a little fellow of his age. He decided to wait and let the bear make the first move. The bear seemed to have decided the same thing. Well, so long as the bear stayed on the bank watching him, Balser would stay upon the log where he was and allow the enemy to look at him to his heart's content.

There they stood, the boy and the bear, each eyeing the other as though they were the best of friends, but would like to eat each other, which was just about true.

Time sped very slowly for one of them, you may be sure. It seemed to Balser that he had been standing for hours in the middle of Blue River on that shaking log. Then he heard his mother's dinner horn, reminding him that it was time to go home.

Balser quite agreed with his mother and gladly he would have gone home. But there stood the huge bear, determined, and fierce.

Balser hoped that when his father would go home for dinner and find him still absent, he would come down the river in search of him and frighten away the bear. Hardly had this hope sprung up in his mind, when it seemed that the bear had the same thoughts, for he began to move down toward the shore end of the log upon which Balser was standing.

Slowly the bear came until he reached the end of the log, which, for a moment, he examined carefully. Then, to Balser's great alarm, the great brown bear stepped out upon it and began to walk toward him. Balser was frozen with fear.

A Chance to Escape

On came the bear, putting one great paw in front of the other, and watching Balser steadily with his little black eyes. His tongue hung out, and his great red mouth was open to its widest, showing his sharp, long, glittering teeth.

When the bear got close to Balser—so close he could almost feel the animal's hot breath—the boy became so frightened that he struck at the bear with the only weapon he had—his string of fish!

Now, bears love fish and blackberries more than any other food, so when Balser's string of fish struck the bear in the mouth, he grabbed at them, and in doing so lost his foothold on the slippery log. Into the water he fell with a great splash.

217

This was Balser's chance to escape, so he threw the fish to the bear and ran for the bank.

When Balser reached the bank he became much braver, and he remembered all the things he had said he would do if he should meet a bear.

The bear had caught the fish and climbed back up on the log where he ate them quickly. Then he turned to run after Balser.

Quickly snatching up the gun, Balser rested it in the fork of a small tree, took careful aim, and shot the bear. The bear dropped into the water dead.

A Proud Boy

Balser, after he had killed the bear, became more frightened than he had been at any time during the adventure, and raced home. That afternoon, he and his father went to the place where the battle had been and took the bear out of the water. It was very fat and large, and weighed, so Mr. Brent said, over six hundred pounds.

Balser was very proud that he had killed such a big bear. It made him feel big. In fact, he felt as big as the bear. Why should he not feel big? Had he not got himself out of trouble in a brave, manly, cool-headed way?

The news of Balser's adventure soon spread among the neighbors and he became quite a hero. The bear he had killed was one of the largest ever seen in that part of the country. It gave the Brents several gallons of rich bear oil and more than three hundred pounds of bear meat.

There was also the soft, furry skin which Balser's mother tanned, and with it made a cover for Balser's bed. He and his brother lay under it many cold nights, cozy and "snug as bugs in a rug."

Fourth of July Night

Pin wheels whirling round
Spit sparks upon the ground,
And rockets shoot up high
And blossom in the sky—
Blue and yellow, green and red
Flowers falling on my head,
And I don't ever have to go
To bed, to bed, to bed!

—*Dorothy Aldis*

220

"Fourth of July Night" from HOP, SKIP AND JUMP by Dorothy Aldis.
Published by Minton, Balch & Co. Copyright 1934 by Dorothy Aldis. Reprinted by permission of G. P. Putnam's Sons.

Hallowe'en

Tonight is the night
When dead leaves fly
Like witches on switches
Across the sky,
When elf and sprite
Flit through the night
On a moony sheen.

Tonight is the night
When leaves make a sound
Like a gnome in his home
Under the ground,
When spooks and trolls
Creep out of holes
Mossy and green.

Tonight is the night
When pumpkins stare
Through sheaves and leaves
Everywhere,
When ghoul and ghost
And goblin host
Dance 'round their queen.
It's Hallowe'en!

—*Harry Behn*

221

New Mexico

Out West is windy
And Out West is wide.
I pass villages of prairie dogs
On every horseback ride.

I pass jack rabbits and sunsets
And pueblo Indians,
And Mexicans in great big hats,
And they are all my friends.

But when the moon comes sliding
And sagebrush turns to foam,
Then outdoors is Out West,
But indoors is Home.

—Polly Chase Boyden

222

PART 5

Boys'
Adventures

Adventure in the Night

Most of the summer, Billy Greer, who was twelve years old, had been sleeping in a little tent, which he and his mother had put under the two apple trees between their house and the woods.

At first Billy had been just a little bit afraid. The two apple trees were quite a long way from the house, and the woods was full of tall black trees. But it was exciting to sleep outside and it was cool under the trees. Except for the night noises, it was silent, too, and he could look at the stars. He liked the smell of the damp grass and of the apples which fell from the gnarled old trees, the smell of the earth and of his dog, Bruce, curled up next to him.

224

One evening, when it was time to go out to his tent and go to bed, he said to his dog, "Come on, Bruce! Come, boy!"

The big, shaggy, black dog got up slowly from the living room rug in front of the fireplace and, wagging his tail slowly, came into the kitchen. Billy took hold of his slippery, round, black collar, which was almost hidden by the dog's long hair. He did not want Bruce to race off chasing a rabbit over the hills as soon as he opened the door.

"Good-night, Billy," said his mother, kissing him. She smiled at him happily and warmly.

Then Billy kissed his tiny, white-haired grandmother and, still holding Bruce by the collar, went out the kitchen door, switching

on the outside light as he went. His mother would turn it off as soon as he got inside the tent.

"All right," he called, when he had reached it.

"Good-night, Billy!" his mother called back. The kitchen door closed and the outside light went out.

It was very dark inside the tent as Billy crawled in, pulling the dog in after him. Kneeling, Billy turned down the top two of the old army blankets, leaving one over the old quilt and bedsprings his grandmother had helped him set up on some flat stones from the brook.

"Stay here, Bruce!" he ordered the dog as he let go of his collar in order to creep under the blankets. "Stay here!"

In a moment he was warm. It was good lying close to the ground. The open end of the tent made a triangle of light through which Billy could see the blackness of the ground outside and the odd shapes of clumps of bushes near the house. Higher up, he could see a part of the sky with three stars, one large and white, the others small, golden pinpoints.

Warm and comfortable, Billy lay there looking out. He reached around for the tin in which he had stored five cookies and an apple. He was glad he had not given in to the temptation to eat them just before dinner. He pulled off the rusty lid of the tin.

The cookies were soggy from the dampness but sweet and satisfying. Bruce moved nearer, sniffing for his share. Billy broke one cookie and gave half to the dog. Then, because that did not seem a fair division, he gave Bruce half of still another one.

When the cookies were finished, Billy decided to let the apple stay in the tin. He might eat it if he woke in the night, though he never did. Then he would eat it, he decided, in the morning before he went into the house for breakfast.

A mile away he could see the headlights of a car coming down Creeper's Hill. Now

the lights disappeared as the car went into a wooded stretch, then showed again as it swung around a bend into open road. Probably it was the Waits from Hilltop Farm, or their truck taking milk down to the loading platform at the main road where a truck would pick it up early in the morning. It might be one of the Carters whose farm was part way up the steep, winding hill road.

Then Billy saw the lights of a car moving
fast the other way, going up Creeper's Hill,
and he heard, or thought he heard, the faint
thrumming of its motor. He sat up straight,
puzzled, and then Bruce, startled by his
sudden movement, growled.

"It's all right, boy. Be still!" Billy whispered, hugging the big dog.

Cars seldom went over Creeper's Hill at
night. It was a narrow, dirt road that
branched off the hardtop to cut through
deep woods. Billy's eyes were wide in the
darkness. His father had once told him how,
long ago, thieves had driven stolen horses
over Creeper's Hill, the back way across the
state line. There were no horse thieves now,
but . . . .

Then he remembered. Mr. Grayson had woodsmen cutting lumber out of the hardwood trees in the twenty-acre wood lot. They had brought in a sawmill months before. Valuable birch, oak, maple, and walnut boards were piled up in neat stacks. Twice Mr. Grayson had taken him in the old car when he drove up to see how the cutters were getting along. The three woodsmen who lived up there in a tar paper shack were strangers and rough looking, two of them in particular. That was probably who it was.

The headlights went out as Billy watched. The cutters did not have a car! That was what Billy suddenly realized. They just had the old truck, and they wouldn't be moving it around at night. It was probably just someone taking the short cut.

Bruce whined and strained in his arms.

"Easy, boy!" Billy whispered, stroking one of the dog's ears. "Don't be silly. A dog as big as you are has no right to be silly!"

It didn't mean anything. Billy was just mimicking the way Mr. Grayson talked to the horses when they were cultivating or pulling big stones out of a field on the stoneboat. Mr. Grayson had all kinds of machinery and mechanical equipment on his four hundred acres—tractors, hay balers, everything—but there was always a pair of Belgians or Percherons. Mr. Grayson said a farm wasn't a farm without horses. His helpers ran the machines, but he drove the horses himself.

Many times, even before he started to school, Billy had spent all day out in the fields with Mr. Grayson, riding the hayrack, the big green farm wagon with the red wheels, the mower, or whatever Harry and Dolly were pulling. Harry and Dolly were the horses' names. Mr. Grayson had the finest cows in the country. There had been Graysons living at the big farm for a hundred and fifty years, so Billy's father had told him. Billy's father and Mr. Grayson were friends.

Suddenly, Billy was very sleepy. He had mowed the lawn and weeded their vegetable garden that same morning, and had swum in the lake that afternoon.

"Lie down, Bruce," he said, and pushed the big dog down hard. He pulled the blankets up about his neck, turned on his side, and, with a handful of Bruce's coarse hair tight in his left hand, pillowed his face in the palm of his right hand.

In the minutes just before he went to sleep, Billy liked to think of the things he liked best. Sometimes he pictured himself wearing a school letter like some of the big boys at the school, a big white "W" on the left side of his heavy red sweater. Sometimes he saw himself riding a new lightweight bicycle with a red reflector on the back mudguard.

Then he thought of catching a ten-inch brook trout in the fast, cold brook under the bridge. He had seen his father do that once. Eyes closed, he could see the motion of his father's arm as he cast, the break in the water as the trout rose, the tight line and the bent rod.

The moon was rising now, paling the white house and part of the lawn around it. A cloud moved fast across its face, and

the house and lawn darkened again. Bruce
stirred quietly and sneaked from the tent.
He ran to a hole under the back of the
house where he liked to sleep. Another pair
of headlights moved fast up Creeper's Hill,
jerking and swaying as though the car or
truck bumped over the rough dirt road, but
Billy, asleep now, did not see them.

A Storm at Night

It was Bruce rather than the thunder or the rain on the tent that woke Billy. Always afraid of storms, the big dog was whimpering as he pushed close against Billy. His coat was wet, and Billy pushed him away before he realized what had happened.

"It's all right, Bruce. Don't be afraid!" He patted the drenched, shaggy coat as the dog trembled.

Billy sat up and bent forward to look past the dog into the night. The rain crashed on the tent only a few inches over his head. Thunder boomed and bounced over the hills, echoing back from Creeper's Hill to rumble off into the darkness. Lightning flashes made the white house, behind the black trees and bushes, a vivid white through lines of slanting silver rain. One flash showed the gravel driveway almost filled with water. Leaves on the apple trees shone, then darkened until the next flash lighted them again.

Hugging Bruce, Billy watched the big storm. Water was running underneath the bedspring, but he was dry and safe. A light went on upstairs in the house, then another. Suddenly they both went out. Perhaps lightning had struck a light pole somewhere. More likely, the electric current had been turned off at the powerhouse in Waterfield. During storms, this usually happened.

"We'll have to dash for it, Bruce! Now!"

And they raced across the yard. So fast did Billy cover the distance to the house that he hardly got wet despite the downpour. He slammed the door behind him and

Bruce. Then he ran to close a window in the living room and a small one in the pantry. He tried an electric switch in the kitchen. As he had thought, the current was off.

"Are you all right, Billy? I was afraid it would rain." His mother held a candle in a pink glass candlestick that she kept on her dresser. "Oh, you closed the windows! Good!"

Billy's grandmother now came shuffling down the stairs in her bedroom slippers. She wore her heavy bathrobe, and, like his mother, she carried a candle. Her white hair hung in two long braids.

"A good thing you are not still out in that tent. This storm will probably bring it down."

"It will stay up," Billy said. He had cut and sharpened the pegs himself, tied the ropes to them just as his father had shown him, and driven the pegs firmly into the ground.

"We may as well go back to bed," said his grandmother. She put up her hand to cover a yawn.

A Fire at Grayson's Farm

Just then a particularly strong flash of lightning turned the whole room sharply white for an instant. They all trembled, and Bruce let out a frightened yelp. The crash of thunder that followed shook the house.

"Something got struck then!" his mother exclaimed.

237

"Down in the village, I guess, or up on Creeper's Hill!" exclaimed Billy.

"We'd better all go back to bed," said his mother. "I lighted a candle in your bedroom, Billy. You had better get out of your damp clothes. There are fresh pajamas in the top drawer of your dresser."

Billy could not find the pajamas in the dark, so he put on the clothes he had taken off earlier, his khaki trousers, a thin gray flannel shirt, and his moccasin shoes with their thick, rubber soles.

The storm showed no signs of letting up. The rain slapped hard on the roof, splashing off the eaves, and overrunning the gutters to bounce on the side of the house.

His mother ruffled his damp hair and said, "Stay up a little longer and watch it if you want to. I love a storm, too!" She left the room, candle in hand

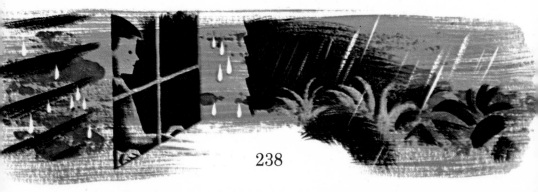

Billy stood where he was for a moment. The lightning had stopped. The thunder was dying away. He wondered if the things in his tent had stayed dry. His mother would not mind, he was sure, if he just went to look.

He found Bruce lying close to the stove in the kitchen, where the electric clock had stopped with its hands showing just twelve o'clock. The dog did not want to go out in the wet, but Billy managed to get the kitchen door open and push the big dog out ahead of him. He stood for a minute on the top step. The rain was letting up now. It was very dark.

Suddenly, he saw a red glow in the sky and the dancing of flames through clouds of white smoke low in the blackness toward Creeper's Hill.

Billy knew immediately where the fire was. Grayson's! It was the only farm in the distance that could be seen from where he stood.

It could be the big house itself or it could be the big barn with Harry and Dolly in it!

Billy dashed for the barn to get his bicycle. Bruce raced after him.

Billy leaped on his bicycle and shot down the rain-rutted driveway, splashing through puddles, and bouncing off stones loosened by the flooding rain. He turned onto the paved road before the house and sped down the hill toward the fire.

A Barn Burns

The rain had stopped, but the moon was still hidden by clouds. Billy, who could hardly see the road, went by memory rather than by sight, for he knew every twist and turn. He pumped hard, standing on the pedals to get over a slight incline. Then he let the bike coast full speed down the next hill, with Bruce racing alongside. Now Billy could see again the tall, red flames. A whole patch of sky was lighted by the fire.

The surfaced road was covered with gravel washed down from the dirt road leading up to Creeper's Hill. The handle bars of Billy's bike bounced painfully against his hands, but there was not time to slow up. The Graysons might be trapped inside a flaming house. Perhaps Dolly and Harry were wildly trying to break out of their box stalls as flames, fed by tons of hay stored in the mow, licked at them and choked them in clouds of smoke.

Billy could almost hear the big horses screaming, so clearly did he imagine what was happening.

241

He was breathing hard now, and his legs ached from the reckless speed he was keeping up. He skidded, making the sharp turn into Grayson's lane. Trees and bushes on each side of the lane made the road inky black, but ahead of him the road was lighted by the fire. He hit a stone, and his front wheel spun sideways, shoving him against more bushes. Billy let the bike fall and ran ahead through the mud and puddles.

Flames roared and crackled, lighting half a rocky field and the trees around it. But it was not the house or the big barn that

the lightning had struck. It was a smaller
barn, away from the other buildings, which
Mr. Grayson used to store extra hay and to
shelter some of his older farm machinery.

"Mr. Grayson! Mr. Grayson!" yelled Billy.

"Billy! Where did you come from? Quite
a blaze, eh?"

Mr. Grayson, hatless, his face dirty with
soot, was leaning on a shovel thirty feet
away from the heat and flames. He was a
tall, powerful man, white-haired, with a
strong, weather-beaten face.

243

"I thought—" gasped Billy, trying to get his breath, "I thought—it might—be the house—or the big barn!" He could hardly choke out the words.

"Just the old barn," said Mr. Grayson. "Saves me the trouble of tearing it down. Old hay mostly. I dragged out a few things. Here, give me a hand with this rake."

Together they tugged a rusted old hay rake another ten feet from the flames.

"Nothing to do," said Mr. Grayson, "but watch the rest of it burn. Just don't want it to spread. Too wet for it to go far anyway. Lucky the big truck wasn't in. Mike

and Joe drove it down to Springfield today with the first load of hardwood. They won't be back here until some time tomorrow."

Billy peered excitedly into the flames. The barn roof had fallen in on a pile of the timbers that had supported it. In three places the fire had eaten jagged holes into the old shingles and through each hole leaped fierce tongues of blue-edged gold and crimson flames. Part of the fire had already burned out. Smoke and steam rose from the blackened timbers on which glowed uneven strings of shining embers.

Boy and man stood on the rim of the darkness surrounding a bright circle of fire and watched. Only occasionally the man moved to overturn a few more shovelfuls of earth where the flames started to lick out along the scorched grass. Billy grasped an old spading fork and dug frantically alongside, getting so near the flames he could feel the heat through his trousers.

"This," thought Billy, "is better than the tent! It is better than a new bike! It is better than almost anything!"

There was no real need for them to stay now. The fire would safely burn itself out. The boy knew that as well as the man. They sat down together on the long tongue of the old hay rake.

"How'd you happen to see it?" asked Mr. Grayson suddenly. "I didn't think anyone would come. I called the telephone operator as soon as I saw what it was so she wouldn't give an alarm. Didn't want a lot of people running all over the place."

"I was camping out until the storm and ran into the house. I saw the fire when I came back outside."

"Folks know you're here?"

"N-no."

Another beam, charred through, broke and sent a fresh shower of sparks high into the air.

"You just thought perhaps you could help," said the man slowly.

"I thought I'd see what it was," said Billy, embarrassed.

As the light from the fire died down, the night came back all around them. Mist rose

from the wet earth and the trees. The hills were like black velvet, deepening into misted purple where spruce and pine took over from oak and maple. A cleared field, high up on a hillside, glowed dimly—gray, chill, and pale. The man and the boy sat together before a dying fire in a world of their own. It was very still.

"Camping out, eh?" said the tall man. "Get more like your father every day. He would have been here fast, but he couldn't have come faster than you did."

Billy Makes a Discovery

Just then a speeding car whipped along the road outside Grayson's lane. It slowed sharply and its headlights veered as though it were coming in.

"Who—" began Mr. Grayson, startled.

Bruce, who had been lying near, stood up growling. The fur rose at his neck.

The car backed away with a stripping of gears and took off fast again, going toward Creeper's Hill.

"That's funny," said Mr. Grayson. "I wonder who it could have been."

"I saw a car going fast over Creeper's Hill before," said Billy excitedly.

"Probably one of the Hilltop Farm cars."

"I don't think so," said Billy.

Bruce had stopped growling, but he still stood looking in the direction the car had gone. Billy listened, but he could no longer hear its engine.

"Just someone turned around in the storm, I imagine," said Mr. Grayson. "Don't you think you'd better come in and spend the rest of the night, Billy? It's pretty late, well after midnight. I could call your mother."

"I think I'd better get home," said Billy. "It's pretty dark."

"I'm not afraid," said Billy quickly. "Besides, I have Bruce with me."

Mr. Grayson looked at him.

"I'll be sending Mike back to Springfield with another load of the hardwood for the furniture factory, day after tomorrow. Joe will be busy here. By rights there ought to be a helper on that truck. Think your mother would let you go along?"

"Clear to Springfield! Oh, I'm sure she would. She would if you asked her! Will you? You could telephone her tomorrow."

"I think I could do that," said Mr. Grayson, smiling. "Let's see. I think I might be able to pay a helper, say, fifty cents an hour."

"Oh, boy!" breathed Billy. "Oh, thanks, Mr. Grayson. Thank you very much. I'd better go now. Good-night!" He jumped up and raced for his bicycle, Bruce after him.

There was no fire to guide him now. It seemed darker on the road as Billy started home again, though the moon was beginning once more to show from behind the clouds. He walked his bike to the end of the lane,

mounted it as he reached the hard road. He pedaled slowly first, then picked up speed as he came to the gradual incline leading down to the Creeper's Hill road. It was even darker there as the road cut through tall trees on both sides. Billy kept his brake on so as not to go too fast. Bruce loped alongside, glad to be starting home again.

All the way to Springfield and back in the big truck! He had often been to Water-field, seven miles away, and even to Bridge-north, which was the county town about thirty miles from home, but all the way to

Springfield! Billy could think of nothing else.

He wished, though, that he were home. It seemed so much darker and very lonely along the road now, and it was terribly late. He had not thought of these things as he raced to the fire. Then he had been thinking of Mr. Grayson and of Harry and Dolly.

"Bruce! Bruce!" Billy whistled to the dog just to make sure he was there and close.

The dog brushed comfortingly against his foot as Billy coasted cautiously down a slight grade in a particularly dark spot of road. He knew they were close to the patch of coarse gravel washed down from the dirt road up Creeper's Hill, which had almost thrown him from his bicycle when he was on his way to Grayson's.

Suddenly Bruce began to growl again. He stood still, even backed up a little.

"What is it? What is it, Bruce?" whispered Billy. He stopped and got off his bike, reaching down to touch the dog.

Bruce continued to growl, though he rubbed his nose against Billy's leg. Billy

252

patted him. Bruce seemed to be looking at
something ahead of them. Billy stared
through the darkness, but could see nothing.
Neither could he hear any noise except the
sound of the brook, swollen with rain, off to
one side in the darkness. What had Bruce
heard?

"Come on, Bruce," whispered Billy again.
He put his foot on the left pedal of his
bicycle to mount once again.

Bruce did not move. He growled more deeply. Billy tugged at his collar, but the dog drew back. Then Billy saw something, or thought he did, in the darkness ahead. Holding his bicycle upright with one hand and clutching Bruce's collar with the other, he crept forward a few steps. It was! It was a car parked with its lights off alongside the road, almost in the ditch. What he had seen was a pinpoint of reflection from one of its taillights.

There had been no car there as he and Bruce had rushed to the fire!

"Quiet, Bruce!" whispered Billy.

Billy pushed his bicycle to the side of the road and leaned it against the wet trunk of a thin white birch. Then, holding tightly to the dog's collar, he walked as quietly as he could toward the car. He stood still once more as Bruce, told not to growl or whine, began to tremble.

This time Billy heard a noise. For a moment he could not tell what it was. He heard it again and knew what it was. It was the crunching of heavy wheels moving slowly over gravel road and it seemed to come from up Creeper's Hill. Breathing hard, Billy listened carefully. Then he saw what seemed to be a moving light among the trees perhaps a quarter mile up the Creeper's Hill road.

Who could be up there at this time of the night—or early morning? Whose car was parked at the side of the road?

Billy, a little frightened now, did not know what to do. Should he get his bicycle and dash as fast as he could for home, or should he run back to Mr. Grayson's? If he did, what could he tell him? Perhaps nothing was wrong at all.

Bruce whimpered low as they stood there, and Billy patted his head.

"Let's look at the car," Billy suggested to the dog. "Perhaps we can see whose it is."

As if he understood, Bruce crept silently forward with Billy until they were right behind the car. It was a big powerful car, an almost new automobile of some very dark color and splashed high with mud. Evidently it had been driven at high speed over the muddied roads. Perhaps it was the car that had started to turn into Mr. Grayson's driveway. It might even be the car that had traveled so fast over Creeper's Hill when he first went into his tent earlier that night.

The sound of the wheels coming down Creeper's Hill was getting louder, but Billy could not hear an engine sound. Then he

257

realized that whatever car was coming down was coasting. The light he had seen grew brighter. From the way it moved, he knew it was a lantern someone was carrying. He thought he could hear the sound of low voices.

That was what it was! Probably some car had broken down coming over the narrow, rutted Creeper's Hill road, and someone had come to help them. Probably the big car he had his hand on had come from the garage in Waterfield to bring a mechanic. Billy did not feel afraid now, just curious, but he kept his hand tight on Bruce's collar. The vehicle and whoever was with it were nearly at the hard road. The voices he had heard were louder. He could almost hear what the men were saying.

The first words he understood made Billy clutch Bruce sharply and drag him down with him where they could not be seen on the ditch side of the big car.

"How was I to know," a rough voice inquired, "it was going to rain? Did I make old Grayson's barn get struck by lightning?"

"Be quiet!"

"Now can I turn on the engine and put the lights on so we don't get killed?"

"You'll get yourself killed if you do," answered the threatening voice. "Think I want anyone to hear the truck or see the headlights this time of night? We should have been out of here hours ago!"

The speaker was the man carrying the lantern. He walked quickly to the place where the hard road and the dirt road met, looked both ways, and motioned with his lantern.

"Come on!"

The noise of the wheels began again, and now Billy could see what it was. A huge truck loaded with lumber was moving down into the road. These men were stealing Mr. Grayson's hardwood!

Two men jumped down from the truck cab.

One growled bitterly, "All the way down that mountain in the dark."

It was the roughest of the woodcutters Billy had seen up on the wood lot when he had gone up there with Mr. Grayson. He almost cried out. He might as well have done so for Bruce, tensing in his arms, could stand it no longer. He barked loudly.

The man with the lantern swung sharply around toward them.

"Who's there?" called the man with the lantern.

Billy grasped Bruce tightly so that he would not bark again. The big dog wanted

so badly to bark again that he shivered in his arms. Billy, wet from the leaves in the ditch and from Bruce's coat, was trembling himself. He hardly dared to breathe.

Billy Is Kidnaped

"Who's there?" repeated the man with the lantern harshly. He took several steps in Billy's direction, his lantern making a pool of dull gold light on the road.

"It's just some fool dog. Probably ran off across the fields," said one of the other men. "Come on. We had better get out of here."

One of the men who had come down the mountain in the truck jumped back again. He put his foot on the starter, and the motor ground loudly in the still night. It did not catch. He tried it again. This time it caught with a roar. Sparks flew out of the exhaust of the truck. The driver shifted gears fast, and then, swaying a little, the heavily loaded truck began to move down the smooth road. Both of the other men jumped on.

Billy leaped up then, still holding Bruce so he would be quiet. The red taillights of the lumbering truck were disappearing down the road and around a bend.

For an instant he did not know what to do. He was about halfway between his own house and Mr. Grayson's. Should he go home as fast as he could so that his mother could telephone the state police, or should he race back to Mr. Grayson's? His mother did not know he was out. She would be upset, and it would take time to explain. Mr. Grayson, who was a little deaf, had probably gone back to bed, and he might not be able to make him hear.

He was about to dash for his bicycle, when a new thought struck him. Perhaps a license or something else on the parked car would tell him whose it was, and give him a clue to the thieves.

Cautiously, Billy tried the car door. It was open! He felt along the dashboard for a light switch. He pushed one button, but nothing happened. Then his fingers, made clumsy by his haste, found a button. He pushed it. Light flooded the dash. No license was in sight. Billy reached for the glove compartment.

Bruce whimpered outside the open door of the big car as Billy hesitated. Suddenly Bruce barked and growled. Billy twisted quickly as the dog, barking savagely, backed away, showing his teeth. The dog leaped into the darkness behind the car. Before Billy knew what had happened, a big man crashed into him throwing him sideways on the seat as he kicked out at Bruce and slammed the car door after him.

Bruce leaped against the car door, trying to get at the man who rolled up the window. But the dog was helpless outside the car.

"Thanks, Sonny," the big man said to Billy, whose breath had almost been knocked out of him. He found the button Billy had been searching for, started the car easily, pressed another switch, and the big car began to move, with Bruce running alongside barking furiously and jumping wildly at the door.

"Better tell your dog to get back so that he won't get hurt," the man suggested easily. He turned on his dim lights, pressed the accelerator, and the big automobile took off smoothly over the narrow road.

"Let me out!" cried Billy, as soon as he could get his breath. "Let me out!" He

grabbed for the door handle on his side.

With an easy motion of a strong arm, the man pinned him against the back of the seat.

Billy fought against the arm that was holding him but he could not move. The big man held him as if he were in a vise. His eyes were on the road as the speed of the car increased. The truck was in sight now. The man let up on the accelerator.

"But they're stealing Mr. Grayson's hardwood!" exclaimed Billy, as he struggled. "I have to tell the police!"

"The police, eh? Sorry, Sonny. I saw it all, too, including you and your dog. I was standing not far behind you. Behave yourself."

The truck was roaring fast down the wider highway into which they had turned. At that time of night there were no other cars moving in either direction. The car moved powerfully, almost noiselessly. The man listened to the quiet motor.

"Nice car, don't you think? I usually pick a good one!" he laughed.

"Did you steal this too?" asked Billy. His mind was working fast. Bruce would run home, he was sure, and awaken his mother and grandmother. Only they wouldn't know what had happened or where to look for him. "Please let me out!" he begged.

"About 700 board feet of clear top-grade hardwood on that truck, 15 or 16 inches wide, some of it. Nice haul for us, eh?" said the man.

They were going faster again, keeping pace with the speeding truck. The wind whistled through the cracks between the windows and the canvas top.

Billy's heart was pounding, but he was too excited to be afraid. He knew the car was going too fast for him to try to jump, but it would have to slow up sometime. He watched the dimly lighted speedometer needle.

Truck and car were sailing along smoothly over the clear road, which still shone from the rain. They passed a sleeping farmhouse, then another. There was not

a sign of waking life anywhere. No other cars or trucks passed in either direction. Billy knew the road. They were headed in the direction of Waterfield. It was half past two by the clock on the dashboard.

"You've got to let me out of this car!" shouted Billy.

"Do I?" asked the man. "You should have thought of that before. It looked to me as if you were trying to steal my car."

"I was *not*. You're the one, you and those men on the truck. You are stealing Mr. Grayson's lumber and his truck too!"

The big man did not answer. Instead, he suddenly touched his brakes, and his car slowed. The sudden movement threw Billy forward. For an instant, he thought the man was going to let him out. Then he saw what it was.

The taillights of the heavily loaded truck ahead of them were blinking red. The truck wavered a little, then slowed. It was stopping, and Billy saw why.

A flashlight was moving up and down fast in the middle of the road. Another car was at the side of the road.

The big car's speed was checked as it pulled up beside the truck.

Billy recognized the troopers—Sam Fletcher and Willis Groves! He knew all the men at the barracks because his father was a doctor. Sometimes they came and got Dr. Greer when there had been an accident.

Mr. Grayson had seen the truck and a strange car and thought the men were stealing his lumber. He had called the state police.

After the troopers had handcuffed the robbers, they talked with Billy. They told him that the man who had kidnaped him was the leader of the thieves.

"Billy," said Mr. Fletcher, "you have had a very exciting night. You may come with us while we take these men to the jail, then we will take you home."

Billy was very glad to see the two troopers. And he was glad to know that he would get home safely. He had had enough adventure for one night.

Roald Amundsen

A Determined Boy

Roald Amundsen sat reading a book in his home in Oslo, Norway. It was the winter of 1884. His breath came fast with excitement.

"What are you reading?" asked his mother as she stood behind him.

"A book about Sir John Franklin, the Arctic explorer," Roald answered.

"You should be studying your lessons," his mother said. "You are twelve years old.

From ROALD AMUNDSEN by Cateau deLeeuw. Reprinted by permission of Garrard Publishing Company, Champaign, Illinois.

If you are to become a doctor, you must learn a great deal."

"But I don't want to become a doctor!" Roald cried.

His mother frowned. "You are going to be a doctor, whether you want it or not," she said firmly. "I have decided it."

Roald knew she would have her way. He would spend his whole life doing something he did not want to do. Roald had only one wish. He wanted to be an explorer like Sir John Franklin.

He made one more try. "I want to be an explorer," he said, "not a doctor. I want to find the North Pole."

His mother laughed. "Don't be silly! That takes a great deal of money and experience. It takes courage and bold planning, too." She took his book from him and looked at it. "Sir John Franklin's life. Hmp! And what happened to him? He starved to death in the Arctic."

Roald reached for the book, but she held it away from him. He hunted for words to answer her. They were hard to find.

Though his family had a shipping business, they were not rich. Perhaps some day he could raise the money he would need. Of course he had no experience in exploring.

But that would come in time. He knew, too, that he had courage. And he would learn to plan.

Roald's father was dead. His older brothers had left home to make their way in the world. Only Roald was left with his mother. She was a determined woman, but Roald was determined too. From then on, he kept his ambition a secret.

He felt he should begin training for his future. Because an Arctic explorer had to

have strong muscles, Roald played soccer. He did not like soccer, but the game toughened him.

He practiced his skiing, always making the most difficult runs. To harden his body he slept with his bedroom windows wide open. The winters were terribly cold in Norway. His mother scolded him.

"You will make yourself sick," she said. She closed his windows with a bang. "Why do you do such foolish things?"

Roald waited until she had left his room. Then he opened the windows again. If he wanted to find the North Pole, he would have to be able to stand the cold.

Everything he did fitted into his plan for the future. Roald had made up his mind to become an Arctic explorer.

Lost in the Snow

When Roald Amundsen was twenty, his
mother died. At once he left the University
where he had been studying to be a doctor.

One day Amundsen said to a friend,
"Let's cross the plain west of Oslo."

His friend looked at him. "Now? In
midwinter? No one has ever done it!"

"Yes, now," Amundsen said. His eyes
were shining. "It's only 75 miles or so."

The high plain was used by Lapp herdsmen in the summer for their reindeer, but no one lived on it. In winter it was deserted.

"We can start at Mogen, the farmhouse on this side. If we allow ourselves two days, we can reach Garen, the farmhouse on the western side. I am sure we can do it."

Amundsen's friend agreed to try. They went by ski to Mogen. When the farmers learned Amundsen's plan, they said, "It can't be done."

"We'll do it," Amundsen said.

278

He wanted to set out the next morning, but a blizzard came up in the night. For eight days Amundsen and his friend waited for the snow to stop falling.

At last they could set out across the plain. Each carried a reindeer sleeping bag. They had no tent. A few crackers, some butter, and some chocolate bars were their only food. They had a compass and a map.

They knew that there was a herders' hut in the middle of the plain. When they reached it that evening, they were tired and hungry. To their dismay, the door and the window had been nailed up tightly.

They had no tools, but they finally got
in. Amundsen climbed to the roof and took
the boards off the chimney so they could
have a fire. It was very cold, and another
storm had come up.

They found a small sack of flour. "We'll
make porridge out of this, and save our own
food," Amundsen said.

For two days they stayed in the hut,
then they skied on. It was still snowing,
and the wet snow destroyed their map.
They did not find the farm Garen.

When night came, they had to camp out in the open. Yet Amundsen liked being in his wet sleeping bag in the cold. He remembered how the Franklin expedition had suffered.

He did not feel so cheerful the next morning, when they found their sacks of food had vanished. This was serious. They hurried toward the west, hoping to find Garen.

The snow was so thick they could see nothing ahead. "Shall we turn back?" Amundsen asked his friend.

"Y-yes." His companion's teeth were chattering from cold and lack of food.

That night Amundsen made himself a small cave in the snow. This kept the wind out. When he woke in the night he could not move! A huge block of ice had frozen around him.

He could scarcely breathe. "Help! Help!" he called. His friend did not hear him.

When his friend awoke, he could not find Amundsen. It was still night. Finally he saw a small piece of fur. It belonged to Amundsen's sleeping bag. It took three hours for his friend to dig him out.

Now they were both weak. The snow had stopped, so they found their direction by the stars. Suddenly Amundsen's friend disappeared! He had fallen off a cliff, and landed on a ledge. Amundsen pulled him up.

They waited for daylight before they went on. They stopped at every lake and stream to drink water. That helped their hunger a little.

It was getting dark when Amundsen called out, "There is a shed." He skied quickly toward it. It was filled with hay. There were ski tracks around it.

"Look!" He showed the tracks to his friend. "We must be near a farm. That means people—food—warmth!"

His friend was too tired to go on. They burrowed into the hay and slept.

The next morning they found they were only an hour from Mogen. The farmer and his family did not recognize them when they entered the little house. The young men were thin and hollowed-eyed. They looked like scarecrows.

A year later they made a discovery. When they had turned back they had been a few

hundred feet from their goal! The farmer
at Garen had been puzzling over their ski
tracks for months.

When Amundsen and his friend parted,
Amundsen said, "It was a great adventure,
wasn't it? Just like Arctic exploration."

"If that was Arctic exploration, you can
have it," his friend said.

Amundsen smiled. "I'll take it," he said.
He was more sure than ever of what he
wanted to do.

The following paragraphs written by Glenn McCracken present a summary of later events.

Roald Amundsen wanted to be an explorer. He wanted to go to the North Pole and the South Pole. So, in the next four years he prepared himself by sailing on various ships where he studied magnetic science and astronomy.

At last he was ready and his first exploring trip was into the Arctic where he found the Northwest Passage from the Atlantic to the Pacific Oceans.

Roald was preparing next for a trip to the North Pole but in the meantime, in September, 1909, word came that Commander Robert E. Peary had already been there.

Amundsen decided to try to be the first to reach the South Pole. With several good sailors, some dogs, and dog sledges, he set out on the long and dangerous journey.

When they reached the great sea of snow
and ice, the men had to leave their ship
and travel on foot. They set up a base, and
made supply depots, marking their way with
bamboo poles topped with black flags.
These were easy to see in the snow.
When they ran out of bamboo poles they
used frozen fish, stuck upright in the snow!
Now they would be ready for their dash
to the Pole.

For several months the men traveled through the snow and ice and through mountain ranges. Sometimes they climbed great ice sheets. Sometimes they hunted for a way through the mountains.

The weather was terrible. Much of the time they could not see where they were going! Noses and cheeks froze, but there was no time to stop. There was seldom time to make lunch. Dry biscuits and melted snow—that was lunch.

On December 14, 1911, the men were as excited as boys at a ball game. Today they should reach the Pole!

Suddenly, at three in the afternoon, the sledge-drivers shouted "Halt!" Their sledge-meters said they had reached their goal.

"This is the Pole?" one of the men asked. He added jokingly, "But there is nothing to mark the spot."

"There will be," Amundsen said with a grin. He went to one of the sledges and lifted out the Norwegian flag.

"Come," Amundsen said, "we must put it up together."

Five frostbitten hands reached for the flagpole. It was a solemn moment. The men's hearts filled with pride. They had done the impossible. They had reached the South Pole.

About the Teeth of Sharks

The thing about a shark is—teeth,
One row above, one row beneath.

Now take a close look. Do you find
It has another row behind?

Still closer—here, I'll hold your hat:
Has it a third row behind that?

Now look in and . . . Look out! Oh my,
I'll never know now! Well, goodbye.

—John Ciardi

292

Ferry-Boats

Over the river,
Over the bay,
Ferry-boats travel
Every day.

Most of the people
Crowd to the side
Just to enjoy
Their ferry-boat ride.

Watching the seagulls
Laughing with friends
I'm always sorry
When the ride ends.

—*James S. Tippett*

293

The End of the Year

A few last leaves fall silently
Asleep on a pillow of snow;
The cold earth is waiting patiently
For spring's trumpet winds to blow.

Will I know it when it wakes?
Will it brighter be, and bolder?
Something winter always takes;
In spring I'll be a whole year older.

—*Monroe Stearns*

Glossary

accelerator

ac cel er a tor (ak sel′ər ā-
tər), thing that causes an
increase in the speed of anything. The pedal or lever
that controls the flow of
gasoline to an automobile
engine is called an accelerator. *n.*

ac ci dent (ak′sə dənt), an
event not wanted, intended
or planned to happen, such
as the dropping of a dish,
a shipwreck, or the killing of
a dog by an automobile. *n.*

ac cor di on (ə kôr′dē ən), a
musical instrument with
keys, metal reeds, and a
bellows. An accordion is
played by forcing air
through the reeds by means
of the bellows. *n.*

a light (ə līt′), on fire; lighted
up: *Her face was alight with
happiness. adj.*

an noy (ə noi′), tease; vex;
disturb; make angry: *The
baby annoys her sister by
pulling her hair. v.*

barberry

a pron (ā′prən), garment worn
over the front part of the
body to cover or protect
clothes: *a kitchen apron, a
carpenter's apron. n.*

a shamed (ə shāmd′), feeling
shame; disturbed or uncomfortable because one has
done something wrong, im-
proper or silly. *adj.*

as ton ish (əs ton′ish), surprise greatly; amaze. *v.*

as tron o mer (əs tron′ə-
mər), expert in astron-
omy. *n.*

au di ence (ô′dē əns), 1.
people gathered in a place
or building to hear or see:
*the audiences at moving-
picture shows, theaters, or
speeches.* 2. any persons
within hearing. People who
hear over the radio may be
called an audience. *n.*

band (band), number of persons or animals joined together. *n.*

bar ber ry (bär′ber′ē), shrub
with yellow flowers and
sour red berries. *n.*

---

hat, āge, cāre, fär; let, ēqual, tėrm; it, īce; hot, ōpen, ôrder; oil, out; cup, put,
rüle, ūse; ch, child; ng, long; th, thin; ᵺ, then; zh, measure; ə represents *a*
in about, *e* in taken, *i* in pencil, *o* in lemon, *u* in circus.

bargain   clapboard

bar gain (bär′gən), an agreement to trade or exchange. *n.*

bar racks (bar′əks), building or group of buildings for soldiers to live in; large plain building in which many people live. *n.*

bay (bā), reddish-brown: *a bay horse. adj.*

beard (bērd), hair growing on a man's face. *n.*

be lov ed (bi luv′id or bi luvd′), 1. dearly loved; dear. 2. person who is loved; darling. *adj., n.*

bit ter (bit′ər), showing pain or grief: *bitter tears. adj.*

blaze (blāz), 1. bright flame or fire: *He could see the blaze of the campfire across the beach.* 2. burn with a bright flame: *A fire was blazing in the fireplace.* 3. show bright colors or lights: *On Christmas Eve the big house blazed with lights. n., v.*

blow (blō), a hard hit; knock; stroke: *He struck the man a blow that sent him to the floor. n.*

bolt (bōlt), a sliding fastening for a door; the sliding piece in a lock. *n.*

boom (büm), make a deep hollow sound like a cannon or big waves: *The big man's voice boomed out above the rest. v.*

bounce (bouns), bound like a ball: *The baby likes to bounce up and down on the bed. v.*

bou quet (bü kā′ or bō kā′), a bunch of flowers. *n.*

bow (bō), weapon for shooting arrows. A bow consists of a strip of elastic wood bent by a string. *n.*

burst (bėrst), go, come, do, etc., by force or suddenly: *He burst into the room. v.*

bur y (ber′ē), place in the earth, in a tomb, or in the sea. A dead body is usually buried. *v.*

cack le (kak′l), 1. the shrill, broken sound that a hen makes after laying an egg. 2. make this sound. 3. broken or harsh laughter. 4. noisy chatter; silly talk. *n., v.*

car riage (kar′ij), 1. a vehicle having wheels. Carriages are usually drawn by horses and are used to carry people. *n.*

cat tail (kat′tāl), tall marsh plant with flowers in long, round, furry, brown spikes. *n.*

cau tious (kô′shəs), very careful, never taking chances. *adj.*

chant (chant), say a psalm or prayer in a singing voice. *v.*

clap board (klab′ərd or klap′bôrd), a thin board, thicker along one edge than along

296

the other. Clapboards are used in covering the outer walls of wooden buildings. *n.*

clench (klench), close tightly together: *to clench one's teeth, to clench one's hand, a clenched fist. v.*

clue (klü), a guide to the solving of a mystery or problem. *n.*

clump (klump), a cluster: *a clump of trees. n.*

col o ny (kol'ə nē), 1. a group of people who leave their own country and go to settle in another land. 2. the settlement made by such a group of people. **The Colonies** often means the thirteen British colonies that became the United States of America. *n.*

com et (kom'it), a heavenly body with a starlike point and often with a tail of light. Comets move around the sun like planets, but in a long oval course. *n.*

com part ment (kom pärt'mənt), a separate division set off in any enclosed space: *Your pencil box has several compartments for holding different things. n.*

con ceal (kən sēl'), hide. *v.*

con tent (kən tent'), satisfied; contented. *adj.*

con tin u ous (kən tin'ū əs), connected; unbroken; with-

out a stop: *a continuous line, a continuous sound, continuous work, a continuous line of cars. adj.*

con vince (kən vins'), make (a person) feel sure; persuade firmly. *v.*

cord (kôrd), thick, well-made string; very thin rope. *n.*

cor ral (ko ral'), pen for horses, cattle, etc. *n.*

cot tage (kot'ij), small house. *n.*

coy o te (kī ō'tē or kī'ōt), prairie wolf of western North America. *n.*

crate (krāt), a large frame, box, or basket made of wicker or of strips of wood, for shipping glass, china, fruit, household goods, or furniture. *n.*

cra ter (krā'tər), 1. the opening of a volcano. 2. a bowl-shaped hole: *The battlefield was full of craters made by exploding shells. n.*

creak (krēk), squeak loudly. *v.*

crick et (krik'it), an English outdoor game played by two teams of eleven players each, with ball, bats, and wickets. *n.*

crock (krok), a pot or jar made of baked clay. *n.*

cru el (krü'əl), causing pain or suffering. *v.*

crunch (krunch), 1. crush noisily with the teeth. 2.

hat, āge, cāre, fär; let, ēqual, tèrm; it, īce; hot, ōpen, ôrder; oil, out; cup, pùt, rüle, ūse; ch, child; ng, long; th, thin; ŦH, then; zh, measure; ə represents *a* in about, *e* in taken, *i* in pencil, *o* in lemon, *u* in circus.

297

make such a sound: *The hard snow crunched under our feet. v.*

crust (krust), 1. the hard outside part of bread. 2. piece of the crust; any hard, dry piece of bread. *n.*

cu cum ber (kū′kum bər), a long, fleshy, green vegetable eaten usually in thin slices as a salad, or used to make pickles. *n.*

cul ti vate (kul′tə vāt), prepare and use (land) to raise crops by plowing it, planting seeds, and taking care of the growing plants. *v.*

cu ri os i ty (kūr′ē os′ə tē), eager desire to know. *n.*

cur tain (kėr′tən), a cloth hung at windows or in doors for protection or ornament. *n.*

dan ger ous (dān′jər əs), likely to cause harm; not safe; risky. *adj.*

dan gle (dang′gəl), hang loosely and sway. *v.*

daw dle (dô′dəl), waste time; idle; loiter: *Don't dawdle over your work. v.*

de li cious (di lish′əs), very pleasing or satisfying; delightful, especially to taste or smell: *a delicious cake. adj.*

de ter mined (di tėr′mənd), with one's mind firmly made up; resolved. *adj.*

dick er (dik′ər), to trade by barter or by petty bargaining. *v.*

dis cov er y (dis kuv′ər ē), the thing found out. *n.*

dis pleas ure (dis plezh′ər), annoyance; dislike; slight anger; dissatisfaction. *n.*

do mes tic (də mes′tik), 1. of the home, the household, or family affairs: *domestic cares, a domestic scene.* 2. fond of home. 3. household servant. 4. tame. Horses, dogs, cats, cows, and pigs are domestic animals. *adj., n.*

down ward (doun′wərd), toward a lower place. *adv.*

draw (drô), pull; drag; haul. *v.*

ech o (ek′ō), a sounding again. You hear an echo when a sound you make is sent back by a cliff or hill and heard again as if from a distance. *n.*

e clipse (i klips′), 1. passing from sight because light is cut off. In an eclipse of the sun, the moon is between us and the sun. 2. cut off the light from, and so make invisible; darken. 3. outshine; cast into the shade: *In sports he quite eclipsed his older brother. n., v.*

el e gant (el′ə gənt), showing good taste; refined; superior. *adj.*

em broi der (em broi′dər), ornament with stitches; sew at embroidery. *v.*

298

en clo sure (en klo′zhər), an enclosed place. *n.*

en quire (en kwīr′), inquire; try to find out by questions; ask: *to enquire a person's name or business, to enquire about a room. v.*

en tire ly (en tīr′lē), wholly; completely; fully. *adv.*

en ti tle (en tī′tl), 1. give a claim or right: *The one who guesses the answer is entitled to ask the next question.* 2. give the title of: *A book that explains words is entitled a dictionary. v.*

en twine (en twīn′), twine together. *v. (see twine)*

ev i dent ly (ev′ə dənt lē), plainly; clearly. *adv.*

ex haust ed (eg zôs′tid), used up; worn out; very tired. *adj.*

far ther (fär ᵀʜər), more far. *adv.*

fierce (firs), savage; raging; wild; violent: *a fierce lion, a fierce wind. adj.*

fier y (fīr′ē), full of feeling or spirit: *a fiery speech;* easily aroused or excited: *a fiery temper. adj.*

fi es ta (fi es′tə), a religious festival; saint's day. *n.*

fig ure (fig′ yər), form or shape: *I could see the figure of a woman against the window. n.*

flap (flap), strike noisily with something broad and loose: *The sail flapped. v.*

float (flōt), a low flat car that carries something to be shown in a parade. *n.*

frisk (frisk), frolic about joyously; dance and skip in play: *The puppy frisked on the grass. v.*

fur nish (fėr′nish), supply; provide: *to furnish an army with blankets. The sun furnishes heat. v.*

fur ni ture (fėr′nə chər), articles needed in a house or room, such as chairs, tables, beds, desks, etc. *n.*

gape (gāp), stare with the mouth open: *The savages gaped when they saw an airplane for the first time. v.*

gath er (gaᵀʜ′ər), collect; bring into one place: *He gathered his books and papers and started to school. v.*

ghoul (gül), in Oriental stories, a horrible demon that feeds on corpses. *n.*

gin ger bread (jin′jər bred), a kind of cake flavored with ginger. Gingerbread is often made in fancy shapes to to please children. *n.*

glance (glans), a quick look. *n.*

---

hat, āge, cãre, fär; let, ēqual, tėrm; it, īce; hot, ōpen, ôrder; oil, out; cup, pùt, rüle, ūse; ch, child; ng, long; th, thin; ᴛʜ, then; zh, measure; ə represents *a* in about, *e* in taken, *i* in pencil, *o* in lemon, *u* in circus.

glare

glare (glār), stare fiercely and with anger. *v.*

gleam (glēm), a flash or beam of light. *We saw the gleam of headlights through the rain. n.*

grad u al (graj′ü əl), by degrees too small to be separately noticed; little by little. *adj.*

grav el (grav′əl), pebbles and rock fragments coarser than sand. Gravel is much used for roads and walks. *n.*

grit (grit), grind; make a grating sound by holding closed and rubbing: *He gritted his teeth and plunged into the cold water. v.*

guard (gärd), watch over; take care of: keep safe; defend. *v.*

gui tar (gə tär′), a musical instrument having six strings, played with the fingers. *n.*

hard wood (härd wůd), hard compact wood. Oak, cherry, maple, ebony, and mahogany are hardwoods. *n.*

hearth (härth), 1. the floor of a fireplace. 2. fireside; home: *The soldiers longed for their own hearths. n.*

hick o ry (hik′ə rē), a North American tree whose nuts are good to eat. *n.*

hitch (hich), move or pull with a jerk. *v.*

hob ble (hob′əl), walk awkwardly; limp. *v.*

hor ror (hôr ər), a shivering,

legally

shaking terror. *n.*

house keep ing (hous′kēp-ing), management of a home and its affairs; doing the housework. *n.*

im pa tient (im pā′shənt), not patient, not willing to bear delay, pain, bother, etc. *adj.*

in cline (in′klīn), slope, slant. *n.*

in hab it (in hab′it), live in (a place, region, house, cave, tree, etc.). *v.*

in stant ly (in′stənt lē), at once. *adv.*

in stead (in sted′), in place (of). *adv.*

in ter fere (in′tər fēr′), meddle. *v.*

ir ri tate (ir′ə tāt), annoy; provoke, vex; arouse to impatience or anger: *Flies irritate horses. v.*

jag ged (jag′id), with points sticking out; notched. *adj.*

jos tle (jos′əl), strike, push, or crowd against; elbow roughly: *We were jostled by the big crowd at the entrance to the circus. v.*

kitch en (kich′ən), room where food is cooked. *n.*

le gal ly (lē′gl ē), 1. in a legal manner. 2. according to

meadow   overtake

law: *He is legally respon-
sible for his wife's debts.*
adv.

mead ow (med′ō), 1. piece of
grassy land, especially one
used for growing hay. 2. low
grassy land near a stream.
n.

mean time (mēn′tīm′), in the
time between. *adv.*

meer schaum (mēr′ shəm),
very soft, light stone used
to make tobacco pipes. *n.*

me te or (mē′tē ər), mass of
stone or metal that comes
toward the earth from outer
space with enormous speed;
shooting star. *n.*

mim ic (mim′ik), make fun of
by imitating. *v.*

mince (mins), meat cut ·up
into very small pieces;
mincemeat. *n.*

mis er a ble   (miz′ər ə bəl),
unhappy: *A sick child is
often miserable. adj.*

mis tak en   (mis tāk′ən),
wrong in opinion; having
made a mistake. *adj.*

moon light (mün′līt), 1. the
light of the moon. 2. having
the light of the moon: *a
moonlight night. n., adj.*

mor sel (môr′səl), a mouthful;
a small bite. *n.*

muf fle (muf′əl), to dull or
deaden (a sound). *v.*

muf fler (muf′lər), a wrap or
scarf worn for warmth. *n.*

mys te ri ous   (mis tir′ē əs),
full of mystery; hard to ex-

plain or understand; secret;
hidden: *Electricity is mysterious. adj.*

new com er (nü′kum ər), person who has just come or
who came not long ago. *n.*

night mare (nīt′mãr), very
distressing dream; very distressing experience. *n.*

nut meat (nut′mēt′), kernel of
a nut. *n.*

nuz zle (nuz′əl), poke or rub
with the nose; press the nose
against: *The calf nuzzles its
mother. v.*

on ion (un′yən), a vegetable
with a root shaped like a
bulb, eaten raw and used in
cooking. Onions have a
sharp, strong smell and
taste. *n.*

o pin ion   (ə pin′yən), what
one thinks; belief not so
strong as knowledge; judg-
ment: *I try to learn the facts
and form my own opinions.*
n.

o ver come (ō′vər kum′), get
the better of; conquer; win
the victory over; defeat. *v.*

o ver take (ō vər tāk′), come
up with: *The blue car over-
took ours. v.*

---

hat, āge, cãre, fär; let, ēqual, tėrm; it, īce; hot, ōpen, ôrder; oil, out; cup, pùt,
rüle, ūse; ch, child; ng, long; th, thin; ᴛʜ, then; zh, measure; ə represents *a*
in about, *e* in taken, *i* in pencil, *o* in lemon, *u* in circus.

pack et (pak′it), small package; parcel: *a packet of letters. n.*

pad (pad), a cushionlike part on the bottom side of the feet of dogs, foxes, and some other animals. *n.*

pale (pāl), turn pale: *Her face paled at the bad news. v.*

pa tient (pā′shənt), having patience; showing patience. *adj.*

pa tri ot (pā′trē ət), person who loves and loyally supports his country. *n.*

paw (pô), the foot of an animal having claws. Cats and dogs have paws. *n.*

peaked (pēkt), pointed: *a peaked cap. adj.*

peal (pēl), a loud, long sound: *a peal of thunder, peals of laughter. n.*

plat form (plat′fôrm), 1. a raised level surface. A hall usually has a platform for speakers. 2. plan of action or statement of principles of a group. *n.*

perch (pirch), alight and rest; sit: *A robin perched on our porch railing. v.*

plead (plēd), offer reasons for or against something; argue. *v.*

pleas ure (plezh′ ər), something that pleases; a joy; a delight: *It would be a pleasure to see you again. n.*

poke (pōk), thrust; push: *A gossip pokes her nose into other people's business. v.*

pol len (pol′ən), the fine yellowish powder on flowers. Grains of pollen carried to the pistils of flowers fertilize them. *n.*

pound (pound), a sum of British money worth 20 shillings. A pound is worth about $2.40 today. *n.*

pre cious (presh′əs), having great value. *Diamonds and rubies are precious stones. adj.*

pre serves (pri zėrvz′), fruit cooked with sugar and sealed from the air: *Mother made some plum preserves. n.*

pre tend (pri tend′), 1. make believe. 2. claim: *I don't pretend to be a musician. v.*

prob a bly (prob′ə blē), more likely than not. *adv.*

pro ceed (prə sēd′), carry on any activity. *v.*

pro tect (prə tekt′), shield from harm or danger; shelter; defend; guard: *Protect yourself from danger. Protect the baby's eyes from the sun. v.*

pul pit (pùl′pit), 1. platform or raised structure in a church from which the minister preaches. 2. preachers or preachings: *the influence of the pulpit. n.*

pun ish ment (pun′ish mənt), pain, suffering or loss: *Her punishment for stealing was a year in prison. n.*

quail (kwāl), a game bird

about ten inches long, especially the bobwhite. *n.*

quar rel (kwôr′əl), an angry dispute; a fight with words: *The children had a quarrel over the division of the candy. n.*

ques tion (kwes′chən), ask in order to find out; to doubt; to dispute: *I question the truth of many fish stories. v.*

rack et (rak′it), loud noise; din; loud talk. *n.*

re call (ri kôl′), call back to mind; remember: *I can recall stories that my mother told me years ago. v.*

re cov er (ri kuv′ər), get back (something lost, taken away, or stolen): *to recover one's temper or health, to recover a purse. v.*

re flec tor (ri flek′tər), any thing, surface or device that reflects light, heat, sound, etc., especially a piece of glass or metal usually concave, for reflecting light in a required direction. *n.*

reg is ter (rej′is tər), thing that records. A cash register shows the amount of money taken in. *n.*

re trace (ri trās′), go back over. *v.*

rib bon (rib′ən), a strip or band of silk, satin, velvet,

etc. Bows for the hair, belts and badges are often made of ribbon. *n.*

root (rüt), dig with the snout: *The pigs rooted up the garden. v.*

rub bish (rub′ish), waste stuff of no use; trash. *n.*

rud der (rud′ər), a movable flat piece at the rear end of a boat or ship by which it is steered. *n.*

run ner (run′ər), a slender stem that takes root along the ground, thus producing new plants. Strawberry plants spread by runners. *n.*

rus set (rus′it), yellowish brown; reddish brown. *adj.*

sage brush (sāj′brush), a grayish-green, bushy plant, common on the dry plains of the western United States. *n.*

sar dine (sär dēn′), a kind of small fish preserved in oil for food. *n.*

sat is fac tion (sat′is fak′-shən), condition of being satisfied, or pleased and contented. *n.*

sat is fac to ry (sat′is fak′tə-rē), satisfying; good enough to satisfy. *adj.*

sau cy (sô′sē), showing lack of respect; rude. *adj.*

scal a wag (skal′ə wag), a good-for-nothing person; scamp; rascal. *n.*

hat, āge, cāre, fär; let, ēqual, tėrm; it, īce; hot, ōpen, ôrder; oil, out; cup, pùt, rüle, ūse; ch, child; ng, long; th, thin; ᴛʜ, then; zh, measure; ə represents *a* in about, *e* in taken, *i* in pencil, *o* in lemon, *u* in circus.

scam per (skam′pər), run quickly. *v.*

scarce (skãrs), hard to get; rare. *adj.*

scen er y (sēn′ər ē), general appearance of a place: *She enjoys mountain scenery very much. n.*

screech (skrēch), cry out sharply in a high voice; shriek: *"Help! help!" she screeched. v.*

scuff (skuf), walk without lifting the feet; shuffle. *v.*

sep a rate (sep′ə rāt), 1. be between; keep apart; divide: *The Atlantic Ocean separates America from Europe.* 2. go, draw, or come apart: *After school the children separated in all directions. The rope separated under the strain. v.*

set tler (set′lər), person who settles in a new country. *n.*

shag gy (shag′ē), covered with a thick rough mass of hair, wool, etc.: *a shaggy dog. adj.*

shat ter (shat′ər), break into pieces. *v.*

sheen (shēn), brightness; luster. Satin and polished silver have a sheen. *n.*

shil ling (shil′ing), a British silver coin. It is worth about 12 cents. *n.*

si es ta (sē es′tə), a nap or rest taken at noon or in the afternoon. *n.*

siz zle (siz′əl), make a hissing sound, as when fat is frying or burning. *v.*

ske dad dle (ski dad′əl), run

away; scatter in flight. *v.*

skim (skim), remove from the top: *The cook skims the cream from the milk and the fat from the soup. v.*

slab (slab), a broad, flat, thick piece. *n.*

slant ing (slant′ing), sloping. *adj.*

slav er y (slāv′ər ē), 1. condition of being a slave. Many African Negroes were captured and sold into slavery. 2. custom of owning slaves. 3. condition like that of a slave. 4. hard work like that of a slave. *n.*

slip (slip), go or move smoothly or easily. *v.*

smear (smēr), cover with anything sticky, greasy, or dirty: *Mary smeared her fingers with jam. v.*

snarl (snärl), growl sharply and show one's teeth: *The dog snarled at the stranger. v.*

snug gle (snug′əl), nestle, cuddle. *v.*

so journ (sō jern′ or sō′jėrn for 1; sō′jėrn for 2), 1. stay for a time: *The Israelites sojourned in the land of Egypt.* 2. a brief stay. 1 *v.,* 2 *n.* — **so journ′- er,** *n.*

sol emn (sol′əm), serious; grave; earnest. *adj.*

sor row (sor′ō), grief; sadness; regret. *n.*

spec ta cles (spek′tə kəlz), pair of glasses to help a person's sight or to protect his eyes. *n.*

304

spir it (spir'it), 1. soul; the immaterial part of man: *He is present in spirit, though absent in body.* 2. man's moral, religious, or emotional nature. 3. supernatural being. God is a spirit. Ghosts and fairies are spirits. *n.*

splint (splint), thin strip of wood: *The man's broken arm was set in splints to hold it in position. n.*

splin ter (splin'tər), split or break into splinters. *v.*

split (split), break or cut from end to end or in layers: *The man is splitting wood. v.*

sport (spôrt), form of amusement or play; game. *n.*

spray (sprā), liquid going through the air in fine drops. *n.*

spray er (sprā'ər), one that sprays; apparatus for spraying. *n.* (*see spray*)

sprout (sprout), begin to grow; shoot forth: *Seeds sprout. Buds sprout in the spring. Weeds have sprouted in the garden. v.*

squeak (skwēk), make a short, sharp, shrill sound: *A mouse squeaks. v.*

squeal (skwēl), make a long, sharp, shrill cry: *A pig squeals when it is hurt. v.*

steam (stēm), give off steam: *The cup of coffee was steaming. v.*

step moth er (step'muᴛʜ'ər), woman who has married one's father after the death or divorce of one's real mother. *n.*

stir (stèr), move: *The wind stirs the leaves;* move about: *No one was stirring in the house. v.*

stout (stout), fat and large: *That boy could run faster if he weren't so stout. adj.*

straight (strāt), without a bend or curve: *a straight line, a straight path, straight hair. adj.*

stretch (strech), draw out; extend: *The bird stretched his wings. v.*

stride (strīd), walk with long steps: *The tall man strides rapidly down the street. v.*

switch (swich), slender stick used in whipping. *n.*

swol len (swōl'ən), swelled: *a swollen ankle. adj.*

tail board (tāl'bôrd'), board at the back end of a cart or wagon that can be let down or removed when loading or unloading. *n.*

tan (tan), make (a hide) into leather by soaking in a special liquid. *v.*

tan ta lize (tan'tə līz), torment or tease by keeping something desired in sight

hat, āge, cãre, fär; let, ēqual, tèrm; it, īce; hot, ōpen, ôrder; oil, out; cup, pùt, rüle, ūse; ch, child; ng, long; th, thin; ᴛʜ, then; zh, measure; ə represents *a* in about, *e* in taken, *i* in pencil, *o* in lemon, *u* in circus.

but out of reach, or by holding out hopes that are repeatedly disappointed. *v.*

tar ry (tar′ē), remain; stay: *He tarried at the inn till he felt strong enough to travel;* wait; delay: *Why do you tarry so long? v.*

tart (tärt), pastry filled with cooked fruit, jam, etc. In the United States, a tart is small and the fruit shows; in England, any fruit pie is a tart. *n.*

tel e scope (tel′ə skōp), 1. an instrument for making distant objects appear nearer and larger. The stars are studied by means of telescopes. 2. force or be forced together one inside another like the sliding tubes of some telescopes. *n., v.*

ter ror (ter′ər), great fear. *n.*

thong (thông), narrow strip of leather, used as a fastening. *n.*

thor ough ly (thėr′ō lē), in a thorough manner; completely. *adv.*

threat en (thret′ən), make a threat against; say what will be done to hurt or punish: *The farmer threatened to shoot any dog that killed one of his sheep. v.*

thrum (thrum), sound made by tapping. *n.*

trav el er (trav′əl ər), one who travels. *n.*

tri an gle (trī′ang gəl), a figure having three sides and three angles; something shaped like a triangle. *n.*

trick le (trik′əl), flow or fall in drops or in a small stream: *Tears trickled down her cheeks. The brook trickled through the valley. v.*

trou ble some (trub′əl səm), causing trouble; annoying; full of trouble. *adj.*

trum pet (trum′pit), make a sound like a trumpet: *The elephant trumpeted. v.*

twine (twīn), twist together. *v.*

un der brush (un′dər brush′), bushes, small trees, etc., growing under large trees in woods or forests. *n.*

un der foot (un dər fut′), under one's feet; on the ground; underneath; in the way. *adv.*

un der neath (un dər nēth′), beneath; below; under: *We can sit underneath this tree. He was pushing up from underneath. prep., adv.*

un for tu nate ly (un fôr′chə nit lē), by bad luck; in an unlucky way. *adv.*

un no ticed (un nō′tist), not observed; not receiving any attention. *adj.*

up roar (up′rôr), noisy disturbance: *Main Street was in an unroar when the lion escaped during the circus parade. n.*

veg e ta ble　　(vej′ə tə bəl), plant whose fruit, seeds, leaves, roots, or other parts are used for food. Peas, corn, lettuce, tomatoes, and beets are vegetables. *n.*

vet er an (vet′ər ən), person who has been in one of the armed services for a long time. *n.*

vise (vīs), a tool having two jaws moved by a screw, used to hold an object firmly while work is being done to it. *n.*

viv id (viv′id), 1. bright; strong and clear: *Dandelions are a vivid yellow.* 2. lively; full of life: *Her description of the party was so vivid that I felt I had been there. adj.*

wad dle (wod′əl), walk with short steps and a swaying motion, as a duck or a short-legged fat person does. *v.*

wal low (wol′ō), roll about: *The pigs wallowed in the mud. v.*

wan der (won′dər), move about without any special purpose. *v.*

well (wel), spring; rise; gush: *Water wells from a spring beneath the rock. Tears welled up in her eyes. v.*

whim per (hwim′pər), cry with low broken sounds, in the way that a sick child or dog does. *v.*

whoop (hüp), shout loudly. *v.*

wick ed (wik′id), bad; evil; sinful: *a wicked old witch, wicked deeds. adj.*

wind mill (wind′mil), a mill or machine worked by the wind. Windmills are mostly used to pump water. *n.*

witch (wich), woman supposed to have magic power: *a wicked witch. n.*

wor ry (wėr′ē), feel anxious; be uneasy: *She worries about little things. She will worry if we are late. v.*

wrig gle (rig′əl), turn and twist. *v.*

---

hat, āge, cāre, fär; let, ēqual, tėrm; it, īce; hot, ōpen, ôrder; oil, out; cup, pùt, rüle, ūse; ch, child; ng, long; th, thin; ᴛʜ, then; zh, measure; ə represents *a* in about, *e* in taken, *i* in pencil, *o* in lemon, *u* in circus.

Acknowledgments

Grateful acknowledgment is made for the following stories and poems to authors and publishers for permission to adapt and use their original or copyrighted material.

"Beto and His Many Sombreros" by Betsy Warren. Reprinted by special permission from *Jack and Jill.* Copyright 1959 The Curtis Publishing Company. Adapted by permission of the author.

"Hansel and Gretel" by William and Jacob Grimm, from *Little Folks' Gems,* published by J. H. Sears and Company.

"An Indian Thanksgiving Gift" adapted by permission of the author, Jen Kost, and reprinted by special permission from *Jack and Jill.* Copyright 1959 The Curtis Publishing Company.

"Maggie and the Little Calf" by Mary Grannan from *Maggie Muggins Stories.* Adapted by permission of the author and the publisher, Thomas Allen, Ltd. Copyright 1947.

"Mr. Y and Mr. Z" from "Mr. A. and Mr. P" in *A Street of Little Shops* by Margery Bianco, adapted by permission of Francesco M. Bianco.

"New Mexico" reprinted by permission of the author, Polly Chase Boyden.

"A Tulip for the Queen" adapted from the original story, "The Blue Sword," by Dorothy W. Stoeltzing, and reprinted by special permission from *Jack and Jill.* Copyright 1960 The Curtis Publishing Company.

"A Visit from the Indians" adapted by permission of the author, Anetta Dolan Krafsic, and reprinted by special permission from *Jack and Jill.* Copyright 1960 The Curtis Publishing Company.

"The Wolves of Lone Valley" adapted by permission of the author, Bette Wilcox Stephens, and reprinted by special permission from *Jack and Jill.* Copyright 1958 The Curtis Publishing Company.

Illustrations: Ann Atene, Ruth and Allan Eitzen, Anne Gayler, Helen and Bill Hamilton, Gisela Jordan, J. C. Kocsis, Elsie Jane McCorkell, Charles Peitz, Betsy Roosen, Clifford Schule, Roland V. Shutts, Barbara B. Werner, Carol Wilde, George Wilde.

Cover design: Phil Rath.